THE GREAT 8

A NEW PARADIGM FOR LEADERSHIP

J. David Harper Jr.

The Great 8
Copyright ©2014 J. David Harper Jr.
All rights reserved.

ISBN: 0986233609
ISBN: 9780986233609

Contributors
Legacy Team: Denise A. Chisolm, David Harper III, Marc Walker, Steve Hooper, and Russ Clemmer.

Editorial Team: Kitti Murray, Sean Lyden

Advisory Group: Mike Hardin, Anne Harper, Dave Heffner, Joe Colavito, Greg Johnson, Paul Ryden, Ron Domanico, Bill Williams, Dick Steed, Jack Williams, Jim Robinson, Nelson Gary, Hunter Lambeth, Mal McSwain, John Fulkerson, and Land Bridgers.

Visit **www.legacy advisorypartners.com**

Published in the United States of America
HarperAndHarperPublishing.com

Dedicated to my wife, Anne, who has been the
love of my life for more than forty years.

TABLE OF CONTENTS

vi   THE GREAT 8

PREFACE

FACT: In life, there are no do-overs. But this fact—the relentless un-changeability of the past—doesn't stop most of us from thinking, "If I knew then what I know now, things would have been very different."

There's no altering history, but what we learn from 20/20 hindsight can have a huge impact on the future. This book that you now hold in your hand(s) is an example of what happens when the repercussions that could have been avoided in the past, over time, become wisdom for the present. I believe the wisdom you'll find here in *The Great 8*, if applied in your present personal and business life, can change what is yet to come.

The Great 8 refers to eight virtues I discovered and crystallized in my thinking as I confronted the challenges of trying to do the correct things in business. Since discovering the virtues and putting them into practice, I have noticed a big difference between my past and present life. I've always wanted to live what I believe. Looking back, I realize I already knew these virtues, probably could have written them in list form, and was even committed to living them in my past. But life itself doesn't always play out like ink on a page.

It isn't black and white. The division between virtues and vices can blur to gray.

This book is the product of a pause. Stepping back, I've found, enabled me to define virtues and vices in clearer terms. It is important to note that just because things appear gray, doesn't mean they are. Previously, I'd be caught flat-footed when a choice between a virtue and a vice arose; but now I find I'm on my toes.

What has made the difference? Daily reflection on the eight virtues and their practical implications to the events in my life and current experience has made the difference.

I now know that if I neglect a virtue, if I allow a vice to have its way, there will be negative consequences. Sure, there are gray areas, but this book is not about those.

Earlier in my career, I looked for the "silver bullet" of success. Every time I went to a conference, I thought, "If I can find it, I know I can achieve any level of success." I now know there is no silver bullet; rather, there is a learning curve, and I have discovered that *The Great 8* virtues help me climb that curve better than anything else does. This collection of virtues is not a gimmick. I have found that practicing them provides the best path toward achieving the life I've always wanted. They give me a balanced view of success.

I used to coach football, so it's easy to see the virtues and vices as the perfect blend of offense and defense. The more our team understood the vices, the more we avoided turnovers and the better equipped we were to keep "enemy" forces from scoring against us. The virtues enabled us to move the ball down the field with a balance of both rushing and passing. You can say that the bottom line comes to this -- a good grasp of both the virtues and the vices all but guarantees momentum.

Business is more than a game. At the end of the day, what gives any business value is its relational capital. The good will of the company is built by its relationships, both internally and externally. I have discovered a distinct correlation between this intangible asset and *The Great 8*. If we are negligent in pursuing the virtues, there is a noticeable decline over time in our relational capital. The virtues, plain and simple, build relationships and good relationships have long-term financial implications - enabling us to attract and retain the right people for our respective organizations.

CHAPTER 1
INTRODUCTION

A few years ago I flew to a business meeting in Chicago, expecting to gain insight for the next year. I was primed to be motivated. Instead, I came away de-motivated. I gained insight all right, but not the kind I expected. All of the attendees, including those from our firm, were several years into a partnership in the executive benefits business through a joint marketing agreement. The leader of the group had the reputation of being a real superstar in our business. At first, we were all enamored with his mystique. He was the picture of success. Whenever he partnered with us in certain situations, the clients were impressed.

But then a few minor inconsistencies cropped up between what this man promised and what he delivered. Now it is clear to me that almost everything he said was part of his proverbial "hype machine." He was driven by ego, selfish ambition, and seemed to attract others who were wired the same way.

The insight our leader shared at the meeting in Chicago was this: He and several other attendees were the "A Team," and we should bring them in on all of our new business opportunities going forward. This, as you may imagine, felt like a kick in the gut. The implication was that the rest of us were assigned to the "B Team." I wondered why they considered themselves the "A Team." Some of the people on the so-called "A Team" had less production than we did; yet they dominated most of the discussion. They seemed to enjoy hearing themselves talk while the rest of us sat in silence, too stunned to voice our objection(s).

It was not long after this meeting that things began to deteriorate and it became clear that we needed to separate ourselves from this dysfunction. Superstar leaders require lots of placating. You stroke their ego rather than confront them. In retrospect, I cannot believe we put up with his behavior as long as we did. The ultimate outcome was not surprising. Within the next two years, all the guys on the ego-driven "A Team" were at each other's financial throats, suing one another.

That's when we finally saw that our superstar's values and ours were not the same. Knowing what you don't value is the first step toward knowing who you are. But that wasn't enough. We had to clarify our values for our strategic partners, clients, and ourselves. There were issues on the external side with clients, where strategic partners failed to complete promised deliverables within the required time. With the strategic partners, we also noticed that our internal verbal agreements were conveniently "forgotten."

Values were an internal issue as well. One of the marketing representatives in our organization traveled to another state for multiple days at a time over several months at the company's expense. Every time he returned, he gave glowing reports about all of the new opportunities he'd uncovered on his trip. At first we believed he was doing a great job; however, none of these trips led to any new business opportunities. The only people he sold on anything was our own team.

This experience drove home the need to clearly identify corporate values for our organization. Bill Straub, my partner, and the rest of our internal team began discussions on these issues. We looked at other corporate value statements, but what we reviewed seemed to be more focused on political correctness than on anything of substance. It's not that we disagreed with these value statements, such as "protecting the environment," "being a proponent of diversity," and "striving for continuous improvement." We couldn't help but notice that these statements appeared suspiciously crafted to create a good perception with the public, as opposed to instilling internal values with the potential to guide people within an organization. With this review, it opened our minds and that is how we came upon *The Great 8*.

For several years, I'd been studying eight virtues that I discovered in the Book of Matthew, which are universal in their application to the broad spectrum of all human experience. Over time, I began to see how these same virtues could also be foundational for any organization, including ours, to thrive for the long haul.

This got us thinking about the terminology we were using to define our corporate values because the term "value" seemed to imply a relative or temporary framework, often derived from the latest buzzwords touted by management gurus. However, "virtue" conveys a sense of being timeless and universal, offering a more dependable guide for how to lead our organizations to achieve sustainable and enduring success.

Therefore, instead of developing a list of corporate values, we adopted the eight virtues – *The Great 8* – as a set of immutable traits to develop in our personal leadership and instill in our team.

Eight Virtues to Build Your Legacy

Whether you lead a for-profit company or a not–for-profit organization, you're very concerned with attracting and retaining exceptional individuals in your organization. So, how do you do it?

Your company's compensation and benefits plan is an important way to align your key talent with your vision. Over the years, I've seen this work. The more effectively an organization designs its compensation and benefits plans, the more able that organization is to attract and retain gifted employees who in turn build the overall value of the company.

Compensation isn't the only tractor beam in your arsenal to draw and keep gifted people. Culture and a positive environment, although far less tangible, can be just as attractive. Values are not always measurable or detectable either, but if anything reveals a company's values it is its culture. Values, though almost always behind the scenes, form culture.

Although it takes time and effort to identify the values that drive an organization, the process is worth the effort. If an organization does not have clearly articulated values thoroughly engrained in its culture, the compensation and benefit plans will not be nearly as effective. You may attract good people, but you won't keep them.

As a leader in your organization, you have already developed your own unique leadership style. You may have reached your position of leadership for a variety of reasons: superior intellect, the ability to articulate a vision, charisma, or great people skills. The true test of leadership is not only the success of the organization while you are there, but what happens to the organization once you leave. In other words, what you leave behind is your legacy.

That's why we coined the term "Legacy Virtues." These virtues in *The Great 8* are immutable tenets that build leadership deep within the organization and enable people to thrive and prosper even after the leader who practices them is gone. As you investigate these virtues, you may discover that they are already a big part of your leadership philosophy. On the other hand, you may discover qualities that have not been on your radar.

We have all observed examples of strong leadership: Jack Welch with General Electric, Steve Jobs with Apple, as well as older turn-of-the-century industrialists like John D. Rockefeller, Andrew Carnegie, J. P. Morgan, and Cornelius Vanderbilt. Of course, strong leadership does not necessarily mean good leadership. Examples of dishonest leadership are more obvious in the infamous stories of Enron, Tyco, HealthSouth, and the Madoff scandal. The leaders of these organizations found themselves on the path toward corruption but ignored the warning signs. I am convinced that their examples of dishonesty represent a very small percentage of corporate leadership.

The issues that most of us face are far subtler and probably won't land us on the six o'clock news. No, we deal with everyday stuff such as:

- One ego-driven person dominates a meeting and no one says anything about or to this person.
- Many relationships within the company seem superficial and lack the kind of transparency that frees people to say what is on their minds.
- People in the meeting you are leading only partially listen because they have so much else on their minds.
- Your company needs to do the right thing in a particular situation, but it requires taking a financial loss, and nobody speaks up in favor of doing what everyone knows is right whatever the cost.
- Someone in your organization carries an unspoken vendetta against someone else, and this is accepted as the norm.
- A strategic partner goes back on his or her word.
- Certain divisions in the company consistently fail to cooperate at a high level.

Maybe you can relate?

That's why I wrote this book: to help excellent leaders like you expand leadership influence throughout an organization in a more systematic manner. The unique thing about these eight virtues is that they are inherently good. You can count on them to build value that will stand the test of time. I believe that if you embrace these virtues, you will help create a sustainable and competitive advantage for your company.

CHAPTER 2
The Leadership Battleground: Virtue vs. Vice

What Are We Fighting Against?

We all know Murphy's Law— Anything that can go wrong will go wrong—a concept popularized, no doubt, by realists. Murphy's Law is a functional cousin to a more scientific law called entropy or the Second Law of Thermodynamics. The world is winding down. Everything is in the process of decay. Things get old. They rust. Your car breaks down. Your computer crashes. People get sick and eventually die.

No one has to be convinced of entropy. At least not in the physical sense. But what about beneath the surface in the hearts and minds of human beings? What about the unseen place inside each of us where decisions are made, emotions originate, and real life begins?

The thing is, even the best of us are not consistently on our A game. Even when our intentions are virtuous, we make bad choices. We get distracted, hungry, tired, or justifiably angry; and when we do, we're even more inclined toward error. Each negative choice we make springs from a vice, from an internal and unseen proclivity toward wrongdoing. I submit that these tendencies inside of us are real, and influence business organizations today. In my study of *The Great 8* virtues, I have identified eight corresponding vices that act as viruses poised to invade business culture, if we allow. Because they operate internally, most of us are unaware of their detrimental effect.

Leaders often measure their contributions to their organizations externally, but when they neglect the internal part of leadership and, by default, act according to the vices, they can unwittingly become the same company's most destructive detractors. The problem is that all of us are susceptible to these issues. These vices are like cancer cells that metastasize in the internal organs of business culture. They are not bound by time and space. In other words, they do their work at the office and at home, 24/7. But what makes them so insidious is that they are not thoroughly bad. A vice is typically the corrupted version of a virtue; therefore, they are difficult to identify.

The Correlation Between Virtue and Vice

How do we steer clear of the vices and lead with virtue?

The first step is to understand the relationship between virtue and vice. Here is an overview of the eight leadership virtues (with their corresponding vice) that I share with you in this book:
Virtue #1: Humility vs. Egotism
Virtue #2: Empathy vs. Busyness

Virtue #3: Attentiveness vs. Distraction
Virtue #4: Accountability vs. Greed
Virtue #5: Acceptance vs. Anger
Virtue #6: Integrity vs. Dishonesty
Virtue #7: Peacemaking vs. Territorialism
Virtue #8: Courage vs. Fear

Knowledge is power, right? Note in the *Vices to Virtues* graph the vices in red and the green arrows pointing inward demonstrate the invasive affect the vices can have on the culture of an organization. So the starting point is education and knowing what the vices are and how they operate. But that's just the beginning. If being aware that vices exist is a good defense, practicing the eight virtues is the best offense. The more you dig into these virtues, the more I think you'll discover that they are essential tools for examining cultural dysfunction and for greater self-awareness in your organization. You will also find that they have universal application. These virtues are recognized commonly in every religious, philosophical, or national heritage. Yes, they are obvious, but are they systematically applied in your business culture?

Companies with virtues-driven cultures are rare. Maybe you aren't a Bernie Madoff and your company isn't on The Scandal Sheet at Forbes. Maybe you're doing pretty well. Nevertheless, look back at the scenarios listed a few pages earlier. If even one of those is common in your organization, I have a feeling you'd like that to change. The virtues, if employed in your context, can act as an antidote to the degenerative effect of the vices, no matter how small or insignificant that effect may seem for now.

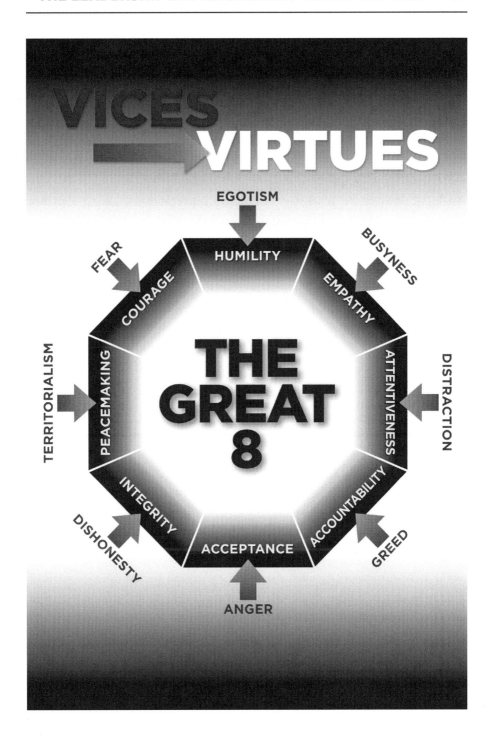

Hope For a New "Matrix"

Remember the moment in *The Matrix* when Neo realizes that absolutely nothing about life as he has known it is real? Chances are that you have felt the shock of that moment as well. For the statistical outliers who never saw the film, The Matrix tells a post-apocalyptic story about a computer-generated reality that controls all of society; and it gets confusing from that point forward.

The old paradigm for business reality, "if you look at it a certain way," seems like the inspiration for *The Matrix*. Fairly static economic factors enabled a matrix of external control. One side dominated business while the other succumbed. There was almost always one clear winner and one clear loser. This market disequilibrium, predicated upon our human need for self-preservation, remained intact for centuries.

Enter the Information Age. Today, the economic factors are so fluid and evolving at such an accelerated pace, the old vice-driven paradigm of manipulation was doomed. My generation has witnessed its implosion. In the past, it would take much longer for the market to restore its equilibrium in the throes of such rapid change. But today's business reality is not about domination or manipulation. Rather, it is about collaboration and identifying the win for all parties.

A Virtues-Oriented Paradigm

In the heat of the battle, how do you do business?

You've probably heard people say that business is all about building relationships. But this often translates into the underlying question common in the old matrix: "How I can get people to do what I want them to do?"

The new reality involves motivating all parties in business by identifying the win-win. I call this a virtues-oriented paradigm. The virtues promote a way of behaving that builds sustainable relationships because it is based on clearly identified wins for all parties. Building relationships based on a virtues paradigm is what I call building relational capital.

If we are to grasp the current market place reality, the eight virtues are key. They help us make sound long-term decisions. They enable us to have honest conversations based on common ground. Our mainstream culture is philosophically divided today, so much so that many feel it is not fixable. But I happen to believe relationships offer hope and those formed around positive dialogue can mend what is broken.

Virtues that Build Relational Capital – and Business Value

Not long ago, I met with a potential strategic partner and reviewed *The Great 8* virtues as a guideline on how we could work together in the future. He informed me that the executive committee in his firm was asked to rank the level of trust they felt with the people in the room, on a scale from 1 to 10. He told me he was shocked at the results. The average score was 5.5. As he sat with me looking at the Great 8 octagon (that illustrates the Great 8 virtues and their corresponding vices), he said, "I can now see why egotism, greed, dishonesty, and territorialism are all evident within our group."

BUSINESS OUTCOMES
↑
PERSONAL OUTCOMES
↑
VIRTUES

THE GREAT 8

COLLABORATION
INFLUENCE
HUMILITY

CHANGE MANAGEMENT
FAITH
COURAGE

CUSTOMER CONNECTION
PERSPECTIVE
EMPATHY

STRONGER TEAM
AUTHENTICITY
PEACEMAKING

EXECUTION
PRODUCTIVITY
ATTENTIVENESS

CREDIBILITY
TRANSPARENCY
INTEGRITY

PERFORMANCE
WISDOM
ACCOUNTABILITY

ACCEPTANCE
MATURITY
TRANSFORMATION

To the extent that the vices are evident, the trust level within the group is impacted negatively. To the extent that the virtues are evident, the trust level is affected positively. I have discovered that mutual trust occurs when both parties embrace the virtues. In fact, trust is more possible even when only one party embraces the concept. At the heart of the vices is our tendency toward opportunistic behavior. Nothing erodes trust more than the belief that another person is only acting on his or her own behalf. Relational capital builds on an accumulation of trust and trust can only be present in a community where the virtues trump opportunism. Over time, people within the organization accumulate experiences that build trust, thus building relational capital.

Note the *Great 8 Virtues & Outcomes* graph illustrates what can happen when the virtues are consistently absorbed into the culture of an organization. The applied virtues lead to development of personal outcomes; the collective effect of the personal outcomes produces the business outcomes that every organization wants.

So, if you're looking to enhance the effectiveness of your team, boost the value of your company, and leave a legacy that lasts, *The Great 8* will show you the way.

CHAPTER 3
Virtue #1: Humility vs. Ego

Learning to Share the Credit

In Greek mythology, ego is all vice and no virtue. Just look at what happened to Narcissus. Lured to a pond by the god Nemesis, Narcissus—who was already pretty full of himself—saw his own reflection in the water and fell in love… literally. The moral of this story, it would seem, is that you can drown in your own ego. It is a dangerous nemesis and should be avoided at all cost. But ego itself is not all bad. An unhealthy, ego-less self-image is perhaps just as dangerous as an inflated ego.

Of the two extremes, egotism seems to me to be the most prevalent in the world. Just about everything in business is collaborative, but leaders with untamed egos don't see it that way. They think, "I have all the gifts. I do not need anyone else." When a colleague or employee shines, this person stakes a claim on their accomplishment, thinking, "After all, I taught him everything he knows." It's not uncommon for an ego-driven leader, in the vacuum chamber

created by his or her own pride, to be incapable of expressing affirmation or appreciation to anyone else. It costs them too much to
share any glory and yet this person can be scathingly critical, using
their authority to make others feel inferior.

Egotistical leaders create an environment of dependency and control. Risk-averse employees may stay in this negative workplace
for a long time, even though the culture deflates and discourages
them. They go along to get along, but who wants an office full of
people who hate their jobs? Eventually, people who are less risk
averse or more entrepreneurial will say, "Enough is enough!" They
will simply leave and start a competing company or work for a
competitor's company.

Leading with Humility

So where's the balance? Between the foul lines of ego and poor self
esteem, where is the fair territory?

To find it, we've got to be brutally honest about our own condi-
tion. We need other people. This is not a point of shame, but rather
something to celebrate. It is not until we acknowledge that we are
essentially bankrupt without the investment of others that we
can achieve a balanced view of ourselves. This is called humility.
Humility enables us to value others and the gifts they possess, even
when those gifts exceed ours and threaten our pride.

C.S. Lewis says of a humble person, "We would never come away
from meeting them thinking they were humble. They would not be

always telling us they were a nobody. The thing we would remember from meeting a truly humble person is how much they seemed totally interested in us."[1]

Humility builds teamwork and the blending of individual gifts. At first glance, it seems ironic that it takes a certain level of self-confidence and security to be vulnerable enough to express neediness. A humble person readily expresses appreciation for the gifts of others. He or she gives credit where it is due, to the person who accomplished good work. This, of course, leads to a culture of affirmation. You can see why people just want to follow a humble leader.

Jim Collins, in his book, *Good to Great*, conducted a study outlining the qualities of CEOs who led companies defined as having top tier and long-term performance over a certain time. Collins called the common quality in these men and women "Level Five leadership." This is the combination of professional will and personal humility. From a personal humility perspective, level five leaders, "Look out the window, not in the mirror, to apportion credit for the success of the company to other people, external factors, and good luck. Many leaders have plenty of drive and ambition, but only a few possess true humility."[2]

The virtue of humility is key to building relational capital in any organization. Truly creative ideas and innovation applications

[1] C.S. Lewis. "Mere Christianity," *NTS Library*, 2002, http://ntslibrary.com/PDF%20Books/Mere%20Christianity%20-%20Lewis.pdf
[2] Jim Collins, "Level 5 Leadership: The Triumph of Humility and Fierce Resolve," *Harvard Business Review*, July 1 2005, http://www.couragerenewal.org/wpccr/wp-content/uploads/level5leadership-Collins-HBR.pdf

spring from a collaborative culture. This only happens when people are genuinely interested in each other's ideas. Humility enables us to forget about ourselves, so we can be genuinely interested in the other people within our organization.

Personal Outcome from Humility: Greater Influence

What happens when we apply the virtue of humility in our lives?

When we're genuinely humble, we feel free to focus on serving others, which builds trust and increases our influence. People are more likely to listen to our proposals and act upon our leadership because they feel valued and appreciated.

As I've mentioned, humility (and its counterpart, ego) has a trickle down effect. It starts with leadership. New employees will discover and even enjoy an affirming culture if the leader demonstrates patience, if he or she serves others, and appreciates the raw gifts the new hire brings to the table. Even though the leader's performance is exemplary, he or she must allow for other's mistakes and forgive readily and often.

Humility isn't an "aw shucks" or "woe is me" quality. These mentalities are self-focused, either self-excusing or self-pitying. Truly humble people are other-focused; that is they are genuinely interested in others, which usually makes them intriguing to be near. Isn't "intriguing to be around" exactly how you'd like people to describe your company and the unique composite of people who work on the team? Today's business model—people working in concert with others using their particular giftedness—can certainly be attractive. But is it attractive enough? If you are going to build a company, you have to attract, engage, and retain employees over a long period of time. What if the "secret sauce" you needed to do just that is not your company's methods or its model but, rather, the virtue of humility?

Humble leadership is harder to model than you'd think. Egotism, the companion vice of humility, is just as rampant in the new model as it was in the old. I've noticed that egotism is obvious in others, but almost impossible to see in myself. For this reason, I wonder if the first question I should ask myself when I notice my relational capital slipping significantly is, "Have I exhibited humility in this relationship?" or "Is my heart humble toward this person?" or "Have I made this meeting all about me and my opinions?"

The thing about a virtues-based reality is that once you finally recognize it, it becomes as clear as the physical reality of a sunset on the western horizon. I find my lack of humility harder to ignore when I entertain the thought that just maybe I'm acting like an egotist. We must remember that this is where humility starts in any environment, in the heart.

Business Outcome from Humility: Collaboration

When you truly lead with humility, you share credit for your team's success, and take personal responsibility when things go wrong. This creates an attractive environment where people want to work with you and collaborate with others because they feel safe that they don't have to "watch their back" and their contributions will be noticed and appreciated.

But you can't fake humility to create a culture of collaboration. It must be genuine, coming from the heart. When Marie Antoinette got bored with her lavish lifestyle, the Queen of France would retreat to the mock-up of a peasant village she had built at Versailles. There, she would rub shoulders with men and women who were paid to play a part. It was a stage on which the queen pretended, for brief moments, that she was one of the common people and that she shared their lot in life. History tells us Marie Antoinette was anything but generous, so while this experiment may have made her look like a leader who shared her wealth with others, it was clearly a sham.

Be real. Your people know if you actually "feel their pain" or are just trying to manipulate them into doing what you want them to do. Genuine humility results in leadership that fosters collaboration and takes your organization's performance to a higher level.

Questions for Application

How have you seen ego get in the way of your ability to influence others? How has practicing humility helped you become a better leader in your organization?

Think of a recent success you have experienced. How can you share that with others in a way that benefits them more than it benefits you?

CHAPTER 4
Virtue #2: Empathy vs. Busyness

The Customer Really Does Come First

Empathy simply isn't possible if you're preoccupied. That's because the primary task of empathy is paying attention. For the preoccupied person, the world is the blur he/she sees on the fast forward reel of a busy life. No fine details, just a rush of light and color. Yes, he/she focuses, but on personal objectives. Personal goals fill the screen so that there is no room left for anyone else's concerns.

When you see it this way, the vice is easy to spot: busyness. It's inevitable. Busyness = self-absorption.

But aren't goal-oriented people the ones who get things done? Aren't they, in business, our heroes?

This is not about goals; it's about the *pace* at which we pursue our goals. It's about margin, as in space for others. It's also about sustainability. If your pace is too fast or your daily schedule too tight (as in no margin), it doesn't matter how much energy you have or how wise your goals, you will not be able to sustain the pursuit. Others may discover this before you do. People who burn out tend to burn other people out. No matter how loftily they talk about "sacrifice for the good of the team," they make people feel used.

Slowing Down to Improve Focus

People with empathy slow down enough to value the people around them. Already, it's clear that the virtues are connected. It takes humility to have empathy. Empathetic people identify with others in the normal ups and downs of life. When someone is hurting, empathic people have the capacity to feel what the other person may be experiencing. When you hurt, you want people you trust to be empathetic as part of your close group. They often don't say much; you just know they are with you have your back. When something good happens, they celebrate the event with you without feeling envious. In the long run, the relationships you build with people who know how to empathize are the relationships you enjoy most.

I struggle with being too busy and too task-oriented to be relational. I naturally tend toward preoccupation. I have learned it is possible to be busy, get things done, and still be relationally focused. I have to slow down and reorient myself when I am transitioning from business life to home life, especially when I reconnect with my wife, Anne. I have also found that I need to start my day with thirty to sixty minutes of solitude and quiet reflection in order to set my personal empathy gauge. This is the only way I've found to be empathetic with the people around me on any given day. My natural bent is to think about all my "must" tasks for the day. Empathy is a choice, one I make daily and it renews my mind.

If not for the virtue of empathy, I wouldn't see past my own day-to-day world. It has prompted me to take action, invest in community efforts with the inner city youth in Atlanta, and to serve in other countries including Zimbabwe (in Africa). Empathy for others has another benefit. It reminds me to be thankful for the opportunities my family and I are blessed to have. This kind of empathy-in-action does not detract from my objective to build my business. It actually adds the value of deeper life experiences.

You just naturally want to be with someone who demonstrates empathy. When my mother was sick and dying of cancer, I remember her saying, "All I want to do is to sit on the swing with Lauren!" Lauren, her granddaughter and our daughter, was only eight years old at the time, yet she had the virtue of empathy.

We often think a slower pace in life is reserved for unsuccessful people. We picture the lives of business titans like John D. Rockefeller or Bill Gates as a freight train, a life with no leisure and maybe even no sleep. But this isn't so. Rockefeller, according to John Chernow's biography, had a telegraph wire installed between his home and office so he could spend several afternoons each week at home planting trees, gardening, and enjoying the sunshine. He mingled work and relaxation in an effort to pace himself and improve his productivity. I believe this allowed him to be more available to his children and wife and to prove to them that they were a priority in his schedule.

Practicing the virtue of empathy not only makes the work environment more enjoyable, it makes it more productive. Empathy enables people to reflect and prioritize. To be an empathetic person, you must take the time to prioritize what has to be done and what can wait. This way, you can be in the present moment with people and enjoy those around you and this approach can pay dividends in your career and business.

Personal Outcome from Empathy: Perspective

So why is empathy in the marketplace so rare? We never slow down long enough to evaluate our position. I guess you could say we're so busy moving, we never stop to consider where we stand.

Busyness is actually the enemy of success. That's because busyness makes us feel productive and keeps us from the contemplative and thoughtful work of evaluating our position. Once we slow down enough to evaluate our true position, we can divest ourselves of our agendas in order to listen to others. I call this setting your empathy gauge. Most of the time, I have discovered, if we will empathize with others and help them get what they want, we can work profitably together, resulting in a win-win.

Empathy may not seem like productivity, but it is something so much better. It is a powerful tool for connecting with people. If we can put ourselves in the shoes of other people, we will discover a depth of relational capital that can't be achieved any other way. Try it once and you will not want to go back to any other way of marketing. Empathy has the potential to make all of our relationships better – with our spouses, children, grandchildren, and friends. Empathy enables us to connect with people "outside of our zip code" – young people, the homeless, the poor, and people from other parts of the world who have nothing to do with business and have no way of reciprocating our investment in their lives. Busyness can't do that.

But you may be saying, "Our business is so fragile. We are way behind schedule. I don't think I have the time for this. Right now there are not enough hours in the day. How can I do this in business, if I know that I need to make a profit, now?"

You've hit on one of the main sticking points in the practice of empathy: time. It is the most valuable currency we possess. Think of your time as a valuable commodity that you cannot increase unless you part with some of it, unless you strategically invest it. It's the old you-can't-make-money-unless-you-spend-money rule. So if you're ready to give some of your precious time to the virtue of empathy, start by asking yourself a question. "What can we do with our time so that we can avoid the vice of busyness and experience the virtue of empathy?"

According to The Center for Creative Leadership, "leaders today need to be more people-focused."[3] This translates, according to a Harvard Business Review article about Blockbuster and Netflix,

[3] William A. Gentry, Ph.D., Golnaz Sadri, Ph.D., Todd J. Weber, Ph.D. "Empathy in the Workplace: A Tool for Effective Leadership," *Center for Creative Leadership,* http://www.ccl.org/Leadership/pdf/research/EmpathyInTheWorkplace.pdf

into an empathy-related skill called perspective taking. Without it, companies are unable to innovate.

> Blockbuster saw the rise of Netflix in the very early 2000s, and chose not to do anything about it. Why? Well, its management couldn't see the world from any perspective other than from the vantage point from which they sat: atop a $6 billion business with 60% margins, tens of thousands of employees and stores all across the country. Blockbuster's management couldn't bring itself to see Netflix's perspective.[4]

As you can see, the implications of empathy in business can be enormous. Like all the virtues, empathy works on every scale, from the corporate giants to the small business.

Business Outcome from Empathy: Customer Connection

Consider how rare it is for the person who markets a product or service to empathize with the customer to such an extent that he or she can suspend his or her personal interests (profit motive) and place the customer's interest first. Once the customer's interests are settled, it is perfectly permissible to ask the question, "Can I deliver this in a way that is still profitable?" You must be prepared to answer that question. There may be times when you intentionally do something without making a profit. You may intentionally offer a product or service

---

[4] James Allworth. "Empathy: The Most Valuable Thing They Teach at HBS," *Harvard Business Review*, May 15, 2012, http://blogs.hbr.org/2012/05/empathy-the-most-valuable-thing-they-t/

at a loss for ministry or social impact reasons. Or it may be a "loss leader," something you intentionally offer at a loss in order to capture future business opportunities. You need to know which of these two motives is behind your choice and not be confused about it. If you are confused, you won't be in business very long. The competitive marketplace is very unforgiving this way.

Peter Drucker, one of the most famous business consultants of all time, said, "The aim of marketing is to know and understand the customer so well the product or service fits him (or her) and sells itself."[5]

Demonstrating empathy seems easy enough. Yet, I am amazed at how rare genuine empathy really is in business and the world at large. In most cases, when I find myself on the other end of a sales pitch, I can feel it, and the "it" I am feeling is that this guy wants to make something off of me. All he cares about is his agenda, about getting what he wants. There is no way to have genuine empathy with a prospective customer if you are preoccupied with your own agenda.

Questions for Application

One great indicator of ultra-busyness is how you handle interruptions. What is your standard response when your agenda gets hijacked? How can you employ empathy in those situations? Have you ever suspended your profit motivation in order to focus more

---

[5] Peter Drucker, *Management – Tasks, Responsibilities, Practices* (Truman Talley Books, 1986), 49.

intentionally on a customer's needs? What was that like? What was the result?

Stop for a moment to take perspective in your ongoing relationship with a current client or customer. Is there something you've missed? How can you contribute to their success?

CHAPTER 5
Virtue #3:
Attentiveness vs. Distraction

The Power of Focus

Acoustical engineers define it as any noise "other than the sound being monitored." It is ambient noise, and most of us barely notice it, unless there's too much of it around us. You've probably asked a waiter to turn down the background music if it's loud enough to drown out your party's conversation over dinner. In so many words, you tell him their playlist interferes with the sound being monitored at your table.

I don't know about you, but I find it is more difficult to block out ambient noise these days, to monitor the one sound I want or need to hear. The information age, at times, feels like a conspiracy to create maximum distractibility. The amount of noise pollution in the atmosphere of daily life is staggering. The data stream never lets up and the vice of distraction is served to us on a platter every day.

Distraction isn't without its perks. It can make us sound intelligent. By gathering information from any and all sources, we can become masters of self-promotion. I admit to being fooled by employees and former business partners who sounded effective… for a time. These people allowed the ambient noise to distract them from the "sound being monitored"—the vision and mission of the company—and it took them so far off course that they did not last. In the end, they had no substantial contribution to make to our organization.

Overcoming Distraction

The thing is, there are things worth listening to that we will miss, to our peril, if we don't win the fight against distractions. I hate to say it, but distractions are here to stay. It's what we do with them that is either a virtue or a vice. So what weapon is most effective in the battle against distraction?

Again, the ancient Greeks, who gave us the word narcissism, give us the helpful word: *prautes*. Prautes has no exact English equivalent. We translate it as attentiveness, but its meaning is richer than that. The root word describes a warhorse that was trained to obey instantly and absolutely, no matter how fearful or distracting the battle might become.

When I was in college, long before the advent of personal computers, cell phones, or fax machines, before Facebook and Twitter, my girlfriend, Anne (who later became my wife), and I actually mailed letters to each other. Every time I got a letter from her, I'd get so excited. As soon as I could, I'd find a quiet place to read it. Then

I would tuck it away in a safe place before I left my room for class. Later, I would pull it out again and reread it several times to drink every drop of her words. Of course, my love for her motivated me, but there was something about my laser-like focus on her letters that informs my understanding of attentiveness. I don't remember the distractions, although I'm sure they were there, because I was too focused on the one thing I wanted to hear.

There's so much information flowing today, but how much of it do we really need to hear? The challenge in business today is prioritizing information based on its value to the organization's mission. To do that, we need prautes, to pay attention as fiercely as a warhorse fighting a battle and as thoughtfully as a fiancé reading a love letter.

Surely you've found yourself talking to someone, only to realize he wasn't really listening. Instead, he was focused on the next thing he wanted to say. This is not pleasant when your colleague or partner does it to you. It is worse when clients and customers try to communicate something to us, and we miss it because we're distracted by our own agenda. An attentive, focused person is rare and valuable to the organization. For some time now, consulting firms have placed a high value on gaining the "trusted advisor status." The best way to gain that position is to develop the virtue of attentiveness. Becoming an attentive listener takes discipline. Some of the most creative and useful ideas I've heard have come from listening to customers and clients.

Sometimes I struggle with distraction. Often when Anne and I are having a conversation in the car, my mind will drift to business, sports, or something else. She will say, "Where did you just go?" Being consistently attentive is not easy. Focused, attentive listening is a skill developed over time. It does not occur naturally. Sometimes you have to get away from the day-to-day battle to learn this skill, and sometimes you have to take the time to tune it up or relearn this ability. Solitude is a key ingredient to developing the virtue of attentiveness. Leaders of any organization must carve out blocks of their schedule for undistracted time away from the business. If they are married, they need to spend time away from the business and focus on being with their spouse. A date once a week and an overnight once a quarter is something we have tried to maintain over the years.

Distraction doesn't have to win. With enough practice, it can be defeated by the virtue of attentiveness and the process of learning attentiveness enables each person to focus on the critical mission of the organization. In many cases, the critical mission revolves around the process of serving the needs of customers.

This of course, leads back to attentiveness.

Truth or Perception?

"But did you see the gorilla?"

After asking viewers to count how many times the people in white shirts passed a basketball in a two-minute youtube video, researchers Christopher Chabris and Daniel Simmons asked them if they saw the gorilla. Yes, the gorilla that ambled into view about twenty seconds into the film. Half of them did not see the gorilla. In their book, *The Invisible Gorilla*, Chabris and Simmons call this phenomenon of perception "change blindness."[6]

We all know what it's like to miss the gorilla and for our perception to play tricks on us. We have all experienced "change blindness." We see a brown lump up ahead in the road and think it's a dog, only to discover it's a piece of discarded carpet. But, an emerging branch of psychology takes this idea even farther. They propose that perception and reality are *the same thing*.

But you can't argue with a gorilla. Whether the subjects of Chabris and Simmons' research saw it or not, it was there, plain as day. That makes perfect sense to me, but if you're not convinced, let's apply Aristotle's first principles to analyze the situation:

> *The Law of Identity:* According to this law, a word cannot have an infinite, arbitrary meaning. In this case, a gorilla is not a ghost or an illusion; it is a big, hairy ape. It cannot be defined as something it is not.

> *The Law of Non-Contradiction:* This says that two opposite statements cannot both be true at the same time, if used in the same sense. Therefore, either the gorilla was there OR it was not. But it could not be both.

You'd think a gorilla would be impossible to miss. However, half of Chabris and Simmons subjects did miss the gorilla. This leads

---

[6] Daniel J. Simons and Christopher F. Chambris, Gorillas in our midst: sustained inattentional blindness for dynamic events, 1999, http://www.cnbc.cmu.edu/~behrmann/dlpapers/Simons_Chabris.pdf

me to believe we miss a lot of reality. Sometimes, our perception gets in the way and makes us blind to what is real. But perception isn't limited to what we see. It informs what we believe and how we make decisions. So how do we figure out what is real and what is simply a trick of perception? The virtue we've been discussing in this session will give us a start.

In business there are two tendencies: one is to be so consumed with our 'to do list' and forget the people part – the relational part of it, and two is to talk too much because we love the sound of our own voice, and we do not get anything done.

Personal Outcome from Attentiveness: Productivity

Marc Walker has worked with me since 1997 and he is one of the best I've seen at consistently executing tasks according to his priorities, which have been shaped by attention to the virtues. He maintains the priority of relationships above all. I asked him to describe his daily process:

Priorities of Daily Tasks

1) Prayer of reflection, "What I am trying to accomplish and why is it ultimately important?"

2) List the items I need to work on for the day.

3) Divide the list by priority and business segments.

4) As items are completed, mark them off throughout the day.

5) Continue to monitor the list throughout the day.

6) When I feel overwhelmed by the list, I will step away and ask #1 again.

7) I strategically think how each item can be accomplished.

8) Uncompleted items rollover to the next day.

9) Process starts all over again.

Looking at this list you may think that this is so common – so ordinary. Peter Drucker says that prioritizing and planning the work is the most important part of productivity and execution.

Business Outcome from Attentiveness: Execution

You set your priorities. You plan. These are vital skills individual leaders must have. But how do you link prioritization and planning to execution?

In her Harvard Business Review article entitled *Three Keys to Effective Execution*, Melissa Raffoni says, "the most creative, visionary strategic planning is useless if it isn't translated into action."[7] She offers three steps for the business leader:

1. Communicate Objectives

> At UPS, quick daily meetings kept everyone on track, says
> Tom Weidemeyer, retired COO and a 31-year veteran of the

---

[7] Melissa Raffoni, "Three Keys to Effective Execution," *Harvard Business Review*, February 26, 2008, http://blogs.hbr.org/2008/02/three-keys-to-effective-execut/.

company. "First thing every day, there was a mandatory three-minute communication meeting to reinforce objectives and uncover issues. This added up to more than four million hours of communication per year."[8]

2. Establish a tracking system to monitor progress.

3. Schedule periodic reviews to ensure stated priorities and plans indeed translate into execution.

Let's apply the virtue of attentiveness to your human resources strategy of attracting, engaging, and retaining valuable employees. Attentiveness can enrich and equip you in each of these human resource functions:

Attracting

As I mentioned previously, you should be attentive to the values or virtues a possible new hire will bring to the table. Are they coachable? Humble? Are they capable of empathy? Are they an attentive listener? Will they invite accountability? Can they accept people where they are? Will they tell the truth both in what they say and what they think? Do they exhibit integrity? Are they peacemakers, able to resolve conflict well? Will they show courage when faced with adversity? If you can say yes to all of these, and if they are excited about the vision of the company, this person will most likely become an asset on your team.

---

[8] Ibid.

Engaging

Want your employees to come alive? Challenge them to grow
and give them opportunities to work in their area of giftedness.
Make sure they have a clear understanding of the financial win for
them and the company. This takes some time to figure out, and it
requires that you, as the leader of the company, pay close attention
to your employee's giftedness and market value. This takes vision
(More on this later when we cover the virtue of acceptance). It also
takes honesty. You have to tell them what you see in them, both the
good and the bad.

However, when things start falling into place, catch these events
and comment on them doing something right. In other words,
make 90% of your feedback positive. This will buy you the right to
point out the negative 10%. No one's performance is perfect, especially at first. Incremental progress in the right direction is the key,
which implies a little patience on your part.

Retention

One of our exceptional human resource executives recently told
me the number one reason people leave companies today is not
because of compensation or benefits. "They leave because they
have a manager problem," he said. I wasn't surprised. Leadership
problems, because that's exactly what a "manager problem" is,
can drive good people away. Again, the study and application
of the eight virtues is an effective tool to develop good leaders
who in turn develop and retain good people. Because attentiveness is not a natural trait in most of us and because daily life

mitigates against it, I find practical tools especially helpful in this area. If you want to improve in this area, here are some suggestions:

Eliminate, delegate, and concentrate. Eliminate unnecessary tasks. Delegate those responsibilities that could be better fulfilled by someone else. Cut your "to do" list in half. Create a margin to do a few things well (Take time to prepare for meetings and get to your appointments at least 15 minutes early). The transition from work to home is critical. You have to be able to turn off the business and pay attention to things on the home front.

Ask questions. Stories are powerful. Everyone has one, but sometimes it takes a little digging to find it. Where did they grow up? What was it like? How many brothers and sisters do they have? What did they like doing when they were in school? As you listen to someone tell their story, make reflective statements that demonstrate that you are listening. Recently I asked a client, "When you had to escape over the Iranian border, what was it like?" or, "Being in India with your dad in your early teens - what was the cultural experience all about?" If you ask these kinds of questions, you'll be amazed at what you learn. You will develop a unique bond with that person because you gave them a valuable gift: your time and your full attention. This process frees them up to share what their needs for products or services might be, but this can only come when they open the door. (By the way, taking time to think about intriguing questions to ask your wife or husband is a great investment of time, thought, and energy.)

So in business, as in any other facet of life, the virtues provide a sustaining influence. They hold people together. Without virtue, an organization will ultimately self-destruct. Like empathy, the virtue of attentiveness is other-centered and because we are all wired to be me-centered, this isn't easy. It requires massive doses of intentionality.

Questions for Application

What do you find distracts you most powerfully on a regular basis? How can you improve your focus?

List your priorities in order of importance for your regular business day. Is there something missing that you need to add or something unnecessary you need to delete from this list?

How well do you communicate the essential priorities to your organization? How can you improve in this area?

CHAPTER 6
Virtue #4: Accountability vs. Greed

When a Win-Win really is a Win-Win

Over five million people watch CNBC's shocking true crime drama, American Greed, the series that examines the dark side of the American Dream. This show wows audiences with compelling evidence of something we all know: Some people will do anything for money. Greed makes for great entertainment on a Thursday night.

But the vice of greed isn't as harmless as it seems on reality television. Greed can be defined as an obsessive focus on personal gain to the unjust exclusion of others, and, if left unchecked, it always leads to some form of lawlessness. It sacrifices principle—and people—on the altar of expedience. When the leader or leaders of an organization are motivated by greed, the consequences can be dire. Rudimentary rights and wrongs get turned upside down in the service of materialism. When avarice rules, agreements aren't made to be kept, but to be broken. People justify secretive, under-the-table deals. There's lots of talk about working toward the win-win, but it is easy to corrupt this pristine formula when greed is the primary motivator. If you've ever been on the other side of that type of win, you know there is absolutely nothing entertaining about greed.

Greed is not the same thing as mutually shared self-interest and it is not, as the cynics propose, the foundational virtue of a capitalistic society. This is an important distinction to make. Let's call it what it is. Greed is self above all.

Sure, every nation has its share of greedy leaders. But, despite what you see on TV, American Greed does not equal American Capitalism. Our country's capitalistic system was founded by men and women who willingly offered their unique gifts to the collective good, who served beyond their self-interest in order to accomplish something great. As a quote attributed to Alexis de Tocqueville, a French political thinker and historian, puts it: "America is great because she is good. If America ceases to be good, America will cease to be great."

Building a Culture of Accountability

Accountability is the virtue that most powerfully counteracts the vice of greed because it means doing business the way it ought to be done. The word "ought" implies high ethical standards. It is doing the right thing, in the right way, with the right motives and doing it in the context of a community that fosters disclosure.

So, building a culture of accountability is crucial if you are going to create a high performing organization. It is relatively easy in a moment of inspiration to say you are going to do something. However, when the inspiration passes, it is not easy at all to follow through with what you said you were going to do. Both the initial assertion and the following action require great care. This is the central building block of trust. If you say to a client, "I'll get the report to you by Monday," when Monday rolls around, if there is no report, there will be no trust. Citing an "emergency" the day before a meeting as your reason to cancel, when in fact something better came up, erodes trust. These examples may seem insignificant, but consistently doing what you say you are going to do will prove to be a significant differentiator.

If you are careful and always do what you say you are going to do, you can reasonably expect others to do what they say they are going to do, even with clients and prospects. When you make this virtue a priority, you're building a culture of confidence. The kind of trust that is built when everyone within an organization consistently demonstrates accountability may not be flashy, but it is powerful. When trust like this becomes the norm, there is little to no need to follow up to ensure that things are getting done.

Greed's Slippery Slope

Maybe you're determined to do the right thing always – I certainly am resolved to this goal. But just as the examples I mentioned above seem small, greed slips into our thinking in minute ways. A little thought that we won't really be satisfied unless we get this or accomplish that and before you know it, you've compromised in some small way. Greed is like an addiction in that it promises satisfaction but never delivers. There's always something else to want.

Greed is a dark vice. It works in secret, in the inner motivations of men and women. The only way to drag it out into the open is accountability. When a group of people commit to helping each other do the right thing, in the right way, with the right motives, the high ethical standards you want to attain really are possible. This kind of accountability delivers real satisfaction, both individually and corporately.

According to the PBS.org timeline, Andrew Carnegie wrote a letter to himself in 1868 when he was 33 years old. In it, he outlined his future. He would retire from business at age 35 and live on an income of $50,000 per year and devote the remainder of his money to philanthropic causes. Thirty-three years later, in 1901, at the age of 66, he sold his business interests to J. P. Morgan for $480,000,000 and was well on his way to becoming one of America's most legendary philanthropists.

In 1892, Carnegie partnered with Henry Frick, who was known for his ruthless business tactics. What happened later strongly suggests that Andrew Carnegie acted out of greed. Both Carnegie and Frick wanted to break the union at their Homestead plant in the Pittsburg area. Although he denied any foreknowledge of Frick's underhanded tactics, letters exchanged between the men clearly show that Carnegie was fully aware of Frick's actions. While Carnegie was on vacation in Europe, Henry Frick hired Pinkerton Security to break the will of the union and its employees. In the process, a gun battle broke out leading to the deaths of ten people. The public was outraged. Carnegie and Frick's measures, which led to the Homestead Steel Strike of 1892, shocked America. I find it ironic, but not surprising, that someone with such a noble philanthropic vision could be enticed by greed, to the extent that he would allow the oppression of the same people who helped to create his family's wealth in the first place.

Greed can seep into our day-to-day business dealings and sour them, but it can also infect our attempts to effect social good with our money. Giving is the one action that can most effectively break the grip of greed on our personal lives. Before John D. Rockefeller became a wealthy man, he gave a significant amount of his money to charitable causes. He lived conservatively, especially when it came to raising his children. He considered his material wealth a blessing from God and that faithfulness to God required giving. However, I believe the lack of accountability in his life allowed his generosity to lessen as his wealth grew. He eventually set up a secret cartel between other refiners, the railroads, and himself. When he was exposed to the public, many viewed him as a villain. He defended his actions by saying he had to do this in order to stabilize oil pricing and save the oil industry from ruin, but the end did not justify the means. Rockefeller's reputation suffered greatly.[9] (*Titan*, Ron Chernow)

Accountability means giving permission to all of the other people in your organization to ask the question "Is this the right thing to do?" This question must be fair game for every person in the

---

[9] Ron Chernow, *Titan* (Random House: New York, 1998).

group if greed is going to lose its natural advantage. This may seem burdensome, but in actuality it leads to greater freedom. The right kind of accountability creates a sense of liberty and conviction within the organization because everyone knows that the organization is going to simply "do the right thing."

The Midas Touch

King Midas has been a household name since 8th century BC, affirming, like American Greed, our fascination with the rich and famous, especially those who get that way by nefarious means. According to Greek mythology, Midas was offered one wish as a reward for his service to the Greek god, Dionysus. He chose the ability to turn anything he touched to gold. You'd think someone would have warned Midas that his idol—gold—was about to become his worst enemy.

This myth points out something most of us know, that making an idol of money is a really big problem. The negative consequences of greed can bring harm to others and heartache to us. It was tough enough that Midas touched his food and it turned to gold, but the real tragedy was that the same thing happened to his beloved daughter when he reached to embrace her. Unlike Midas, when we are greedy, the consequences aren't always as immediate or as obvious. But there are indeed consequences.

In real life, the most dangerous aspect of greed is that it drives a relational wedge between you and your employees, and it can do the same thing between your company and its customers. Because your employees and customers are not likely to be brutally honest with you, this may happen without you ever having a clue. In fact, the more you alienate people with your greed, the less likely they will be to tell you that's exactly what you've done. You become something you never wanted to become.

When greed overtakes you, what you need most is a mirror, but greed often makes the people around you, even your family, put the mirrors away.

So in the absence of any evidence that your greed is a problem, how do you recognize that the problem exists at all?

"If I am paying a competitive compensation package, I can be assured that I do not have a greed problem – right? What else is there, anyway?"

Here is the number one question employees, especially young people, are asking today: "If I work for this company, what kind of lifestyle can I expect?" Most people not only want an answer to this question for the present, they want to know how it will be answered in the future. In today's business world compensation and benefits alone will not retain the kind of people you want, no matter how much you pay them.

Lifestyle is the incentive of our day. Some of these will sound familiar to you, but here are some lifestyle questions to consider:

Are our people working in their area of giftedness?

Do our people feel inspired? (Help them find it. If they find inspiration in the right way, they will treat customers the right way.)

Are all of us in the transformational process of living out the virtues? (Coach them up. Help them find a way to accomplish their calling in life and be good at it.)

What does their workweek look like? Is it balanced?

In their specific family situation, can they make ends meet?

Do they have time for their family, for recreation, for proper exercise?

In essence they want the same things you want. So it all comes back to the earlier virtue: empathy. You're asking of others the same questions you ask for yourself. If you ask these questions, in a sense you will treat them like family. You will bring them into the discussion and explore what you can create together. Even in large companies, you make the company feel intimate when this message flows through your leadership team down to their respective teams.

Maybe you're at a place where this approach sounds impractical, even overwhelming. You can't help but think these concerns go way beyond your responsibility as an employer. You've already invested huge amounts of time and resources, and now I'm telling you to invest more. You have suffered enough already in business, and you're wondering when ownership will have its rewards.

It's true your employees may never realize or appreciate the price you've paid. But it's also true that most business owners stop right there, stuck on themselves and the spoils of ownership.

Do you hear that sound? It is the unmistakable voice of greed.

No accountability equals no self-awareness. So what happens with employees? They leave hoping to find a place where there is truly a win-win culture of accountability. You, on the other hand, have invited the input of others, and you're open to making changes based on the virtues. So think about it. Today you are learning something a greedy person may never learn no matter how much experience they have in business. If you strategize to create a compelling lifestyle for your employees, you won't lose your competitive edge; instead, you'll sharpen it. If something is right, it is not only right for other people, it is right for you as well.

Setting aside your own greed in order to offer lifestyle incentives will ultimately attract great people who will stay on your team. It is the "right thing" to do. Which means it's going to be a battle. Accountability recognizes that the war against greed begins on a personal, heart level. If we don't win this battle in our own hearts and lives, we will never win it in our businesses or our homes.

Personal Outcome from Accountability: Wisdom

In his Harvard Business Review article with the telling title *Doing the Right Thing or Making a Profit – Which Comes First?*, Eric J. McNulty references Mitch Tyson's reasons for offering health insurance to his employees.

Tyson said that he thought about what he would say to his own family if asked about why his company insured its workers. If it was for purely selfish reasons, that would send one message. If it was because it was the right thing to do, that would send a very different message.[10]

McNulty's article tracks the personal growth of a business leader. That's exactly what happens when you set out to do the right thing for the right reasons: you grow. When your intentions play out in an organization that holds you to them, the potential for business acumen is both deep and wide. Mitch Tyson started out caring for nothing but the bottom line in his field, clean energy. Over time, McNulty writes, he "came to realize that why is an essential part of the equation for long-term success and impact."[11] In other words, the right motive makes a difference.

Business Outcome from Accountability: Sustainable Performance

"Knowledge comes, but wisdom lingers," wrote Alfred Lord Tennyson.[12] Maybe that's the biggest difference between the two: sustainability. When you create a culture of accountability in order to ensure your organization does the right things, the right way,

---

[10] Eric J. McNulty, "Doing the Right Thing or Making a Profit – Which Comes First?," *Harvard Business Review*, February 18, 2013, http://blogs.hbr.org/2013/02/doing-the-right-thing-or-makin/.

[11] Ibid.

[12] Alfred Lord Tennyson, *Locksley Hall*, Poetry Foundation, http://www.poetryfoundation.org/poem/174629.

with the right motives, you may experience losses along the way. But, in the end, you'll gain business acumen, or wisdom, from your experience with those very losses. The benefit is that wisdom leads ultimately to sustainable performance.

Knowledge is all about facts, but wisdom connects facts to real life. Smart people may impress you with their knowledge, but wise people get things done. The same goes for companies. Accountability makes for performance that's not only sustainable, but also quantifiable. You'll be able to count a certain number of meetings, products sold, or customers secured.

Questions for Application

Are you accountable to anyone right now? Is there anyone who asks, "Is this the right thing to do?" Who can you invite into a circle of accountability? In your personal life? In your company?

Who do you know who is genuinely wise, who has business acumen? How did they get that way? If you do not know, or want to refresh your memory, schedule lunch with them and ask to chat about his/her business acumen.

What are some measurable ways you have seen your business perform over time? What do you hope to see as a result of accountability in the future?

CHAPTER 7
Virtue #5: Acceptance vs. Anger

More Than Mr. Nice Guy

Most days I'm a pretty nice guy. But nice guys finish last, don't they?

You've probably heard a coach say something like "You just need to get mad" or "get fired up" to his players. At best, that's locker room language for "act like this game matters to you." I get that. Nice guys don't have what it takes, if what it takes is a razor sharp competitive edge. You know, the eye of the tiger and all that.

But I wonder about myself when I get fired up. Sometimes it feels really good to get angry. Anger feels like productivity. It's the same thing we said about busyness. When I'm angry I'm focused and even having fun. But if I stop and look at the other guy, the one across the table getting a bucketful of my "focus," I wonder if my brief anger high is really worth it. Because what feels like fun to me feels like rejection to him. I should know. I've been that guy, too.

So, does that mean I should make it my chief goal in life to be nice all the time?

Let's say a deal didn't go through, or client is being acquired and we could lose our position with them, or we made a mistake and the client is upset with us. For whatever reason, our company is not making the progress we should be making. I typically react to these scenarios by asking myself, "What are we doing wrong?"

This is where I get into trouble.

Of course I give myself the benefit of the doubt and evaluate my performance favorably. I am the good guy. I tend to over value my contributions to the effort and under value everyone else's. So who's to blame if something goes wrong? Surely it's not me. The blame factor doesn't go away, it just becomes justification for my anger. Pretty soon my anger is all that's left as my leverage to solve the problem. Hence, I "get fired up" and "focused" and, who knows, a few heads may roll.

I've observed that I'm not the only one who operates like this. In the insurance business it usually happens between the sales guys and the underwriters who reject their sales opportunity. Or the claims people reject a claim and the client is ready to bail. In manufacturing, the sales guys make promises that manufacturing and operations cannot keep. Because none of us is perfect and no business runs perfectly, there's always someone out there to blame.

My own self-righteousness fuels my anger. I ask myself, "Why can't they be like me? Why can't they see it the way I see it?" Often this line of reasoning devolves into the broader question: "Why isn't the machine working like it's supposed to?" Which makes the person I'm angry at nothing more than a cog in the machinery of my business.

But people are not objects. One fundamental difference between people and objects lies in their discoverability. If a boulder is blocking your way in a mountain pass, you will have to ask certain questions to discover what the boulder is and how to move it. You'll ask "what" questions: What are its dimensions? What does it weigh? What material is it made of?

But if a person is in your way in business, you will need to ask a different set of questions. The "who" questions. You'll need to know who the person is and what his/her story is in life. You can be nice on the surface toward someone you do not know. But that isn't acceptance. Acceptance requires taking the time to discover who a person really is and accepting that person right where he/she is at that time and place.

The Power of Acceptance

What does the virtue of acceptance have to do with displacing the vice of anger? By acceptance, I do not mean we simply resign ourselves to certain people sitting in the path of progress like immovable boulders. I do not mean we accept other people's bad behavior or poor performance. I do mean, however, that we accept the person.

In a culture of high accountability, there are going to be times—many of them, if you are still building the culture—when people fail to meet your expectations and your anger may be justifiable. But if I consider that people are more than obstacles or problems, I will be less likely to put them in the "I'm done with you!" category. This alone goes a long way toward controlling what moments before was an uncontrollable anger.

Anger as an emotion in and of itself is not bad, as long as it is properly categorized and controlled. Anger, such as righteous indignation can be appropriate. Controlled anger can be very motivational.

The virtue of acceptance is the best defense against the vice of anger. The key to acceptance is meeting people where they are – not where you think they should be. You can accept a person without accepting his or her behavior or beliefs. One of the keys to the virtue of acceptance is the ability to discern emerging positive giftedness or talents in a person under your authority and articulating this in a good way.

Over the years, there have been plenty of opportunities in our organization for me to get angry and write people off. Marc Walker joined our company in 1998 as a young man in his mid-twenties. He had worked with me for approximately twelve months when I began to realize things were not going well. We were in a "make or break position" that year, but we hung in there together. I saw a bulldog quality of perseverance in him, and I told him that. I also asked him to stick it out with me and I am glad that he did. Now, fourteen years later, I've watched him develop into one of the most gifted client services individuals I've ever known. He embraced my words back then and became a critical leader on our team.

Anger can lead to rejection in an employee who does not handle criticism by his employer well, even if that criticism is constructive. Often this employee feels he or she must hold onto the offense, nursing it, because to let go would be to let the offending party off the hook. The result is a deeper, more settled form of anger: bitterness. Bitterness harms the offended much more than it injures the offender. The only antidote to bitterness is direct and careful confrontation. Instead of avoiding the critical employer, the employee must move toward him or her. This is where it can get tricky.

Yes, the employee can and should express his or her feelings, but this must be accompanied by a humble willingness to listen and make personal adjustments. When an offended person does not go through this prescribed process, the quality of the relationship suffers. Obviously, this hinders the functionality of the organization.

Expanding Your Vision

Acceptance creates a culture of discoverability. Leaders who accept others catch early indications of giftedness. They are experts at articulating these gifts in a way that offers a constructive path to improved performance.

Four years ago, we retained a new employee, Denise Chisolm, who had a background as a compliance officer, but did not have marketing experience or direct interaction with clients. Once I saw her interacting with prospective clients, I knew that she had the giftedness to be really good in marketing. When I expressed this to her for the first time, she was excited but had difficulty believing me. She had experienced a conflict incidence with a client that made her uncomfortable about future interactions. But over time, she grasped her giftedness and became more confident in her role. Now she is very enthusiastic about this new level of self-discovery and extremely proficient in her enhanced role within our company.

Our natural tendency is to categorize people quickly. If they meet our criteria, we accept them. If they do not, we reject them. Sometimes in business we have to make quick decisions, but if a decision is fundamentally self-protective, it may lead us to reject others. This angry and close-minded approach is very limiting. If we only surround ourselves with people who agree with us, we miss out on multi-faceted perspectives that can make a difference between success and failure. Different perspectives often lead to breakthroughs in innovation.

However, genuine acceptance is rare! Just turn on any cable news network to see an example of what unacceptance looks like. It seems today that our political arguments focus exclusively on proving that the other side is wrong. There seems to be no desire to find areas of agreement. I sense that the current political logjam could be broken if there was a greater degree of acceptance among our nation's leaders. It is possible to accept a person and disagree with him or her at the same time. It should be noted that acceptance should not be equated to acquiescence. In order to gain acceptance, one should not give in to that which is not right. One may listen to the other person and then discern the validity of what he or she is saying. If it is correct, acknowledge it; if it is incorrect, it is appropriate to point that out. Acceptance does not exclude discussions about deeply held areas of disagreement. There are times we feel reluctant to offer the olive branch of acceptance for fear that we will appear to be softening our position, when in fact, exploring our dissimilarities foster better relationships of mutual acceptance.

In his *Seven Habits of Highly Effective People*, Stephen Covey explains the primary strategy of acceptance is to "seek first to understand, then to be understood."[13] In any high accountability organization, it is important that everyone understands that the rejection of an action is not rejection of a person.

Rejection focused on the actions of the person is justified and appropriate in two areas: underperformance and immoral behavior. Underperformance, when clearly identified, is often managed with corrective action. Moral misbehavior is a more delicate matter in that it usually involves broken trust in relationships. But even this is not irredeemable when it happens in your organization. It starts with confrontation, followed by reconciliation, in which, ideally, the guilty party accepts responsibility, owns up to the bad decision, and commits to different behavior. Then acceptance

---

[13] Stephen Covey, "Habit 5: Seek First to Understand, Then to be Understood," *www.stephencovey.com*, https://www.stephencovey.com/7habits/7habits-habit5.php.

offered by the offended party creates the opportunity for forgiveness. Underperformance and moral lapses should be handled as quickly as possible. In some cases, the guilty party fails to accept responsibility and does not own up to the bad decision, and does not commit to different behavior. When this happens, the person must leave the organization.

I have observed that good leaders are transparent about their own failures and readily admit to them. It is easy to see the guilt in others, but it is much harder to admit our own guilt, especially when someone has offended us. If one person takes the lead and demonstrates a willingness to admit guilt, make restitution, and ask for forgiveness, it breathes life into others in the organization.

The virtue of acceptance leads to a culture where there are few hidden agendas or simmering undercurrents. Uncontrolled anger, on the other hand, sucks the energy out of a culture. Acceptance infuses the culture with energy. Acceptance allows for personal discovery and innovation to emerge so that people can function at their highest level. Again, the virtues build upon one another. It takes humility, empathy, attentiveness, and accountability to demonstrate the virtue of acceptance.

Personal Outcome from Acceptance: Maturity

It may have been the most bizarre tantrum ever thrown in a public forum. A very intoxicated (he admitted later) Kanye West interrupted Taylor Swift's acceptance speech at the 2009 MTV Music Awards to tell her, and the world, that he felt she did not deserve it. Millions chuckled at West's childish display, wondering how a grown man could be so immature. But no one was surprised. Like greed, fame does ridiculous things to people. It can lock them in childhood so that they are about as nice to be around as a tired, hungry two-year-old.

As I said earlier, most days I'm a pretty nice guy. A nice guy who can justify my anger if I'm not careful. Besides, isn't throwing a public tantrum ala Kanye West anything to brag about? Is "nice" all I want for myself personally or the people in my company? Acceptance is far more substantial than nice. Nice is a social convention, but acceptance is not only the way to mature personally; it is a powerful way to build genuine social capital.

Business Outcome from Acceptance: Team Transformation

Believe it or not, acceptance could very well unlock something magical in your company. This is possible only when we remember that people are not static objects. That means everything they do and say is part of their dynamic, ever-changing story. The pathway to genuine acceptance begins with discovering, not just a person's identity, but where they are in their personal story.

What if the sales person is an extrovert who talks too much and makes unrealistic promises? Or he tends to want to get the deal so badly that he is afraid to negotiate adequate pricing.

What if you get a bad report from a client about one of your service people? The client is unhappy and rather than owning up to our responsibility in the problem, the service person wants to blame the customer. The pathway to genuine acceptance begins with discovering, not just a person's identity, but where they are in their story.

You may have a CFO who has a doomsday perspective, who is always resisting your visions and is unyielding in his position. What do you do as CEO? To get to acceptance, you must know the person first. You must discover who he or she is at a personal level.

I have developed the following list of questions, an Acceptance Inventory, to help me in this discovery process:

1. Why did I hire him/her in the first place?

2. What in his/her life experience is making him/her underperform?

3. What area of giftedness does he/she bring to the table?

4. How does he/she know when they are "on" – working in their sweet spot?

5. Is he/she still a good fit in what we are trying to do?

6. Is he/she open to being coached? Will he/she listen?

7. What exactly do I want him/her to do now?

8. Have I been clear in articulating my expectations?

When I step back and thoughtfully consider these questions about a person in our company, I not only discover who he/she really is, I also discover the correct course of action. Sometimes he/she can't stay. You have to be willing to face this reality. It may be that the best thing for him/her and the company is for this person to go. If they are going to stay on the team, I need to proclaim the truth in advance - I need to proclaim his/her emerging giftedness and the improved actions I see in the future. I tell him/her how to grow in performance.

To the sales person who talks too much and makes unrealistic promises, I might say, "Remember the reason you came on with us. You love being with people and you have the ability to forge long term business relationships; and if you could take the time to ask these specific questions and envision the ideal solution for the customer and for us, I think you could take your marketing to a new level of competence." Then I would define in detail what the questions should be and what the ideal solutions should be.

To the service person who wants to blame the customer I might say, "Here is what I have noticed about you. You have demonstrated an ability to win people over through persevering though situations like this. The client perspective is what it is. I don't want to hear any more about the customer being the problem. I can see you working through this and ultimately winning them over and building a stronger relationship with them than what you have had previously."

To the CFO who always seems to resist your visions and is unyielding in his position I might say, "The reason why you are here is because you bring financial accountability to our company, and we need that. I also need you to work with me on these optimistic visions and figure out how we can make this happen in a fiscally sound way. I can see you doing that for us."

Proclaiming the truth in advance is the best way to gain improved performance in your people. This is the final function of acceptance. Not only does acceptance affirm someone's identity, it gives him or her hope for the next chapter in his or her story.

Questions for Application

What makes you really angry? Has this changed over time? Can you think of a time when you chose to accept someone who initially made you angry?

What does maturity look like to you? And how is it much more complex and nuanced than simply being a nice guy?

Think of someone in your organization and describe his or her story. Have you discovered his or her unique giftedness? If not, how can you do that in the future?

CHAPTER 8
Virtue #6: Integrity vs. Dishonesty

Can You See Through Me?

The color of self-deception is not black or white; it's gray. This makes it hard to see in me. But trust me; it is there. It's so subtle yet unmistakable. How easily I find I can manipulate a situation in my favor or how I can become a chameleon by acting a certain way with a group of people I want to impress! If you're honest, I know you recognize this hint of gray in your own life. If you sell a product or service, you find it necessary to tell a compelling story by overstating your case, by promising big when you know you can only deliver small.

I have news for you. Customers and clients can see right through us. What looks gray to us is clear to them, and when we lie, no matter how small the misrepresentation of the truth, it undermines our trusted advisor status. A person of integrity is consistent in his actions, no matter the company he keeps. He tells the truth and nothing but the truth. He is confident in the truth. He avoids statements that create a false impression. Integrity leads to greater credibility because you deliver on what you promise. Integrity builds security and longevity in an organization because everyone is committed to doing the right thing. The dishonest person lives with a constant, low-grade fear that the skeleton of lies, no matter how small, will be found out. The person of integrity travels light. No reason to fear. Integrity enables an organization to weather the storms of adversity and protect its brand.

Transparency (and Vulnerability)

Once you start focusing on integrity, you notice its absence even more. The ironic thing is that the moment someone makes a bold assertion about his or her perfect integrity, we immediately know he/she probably has very little.

At a public debate, a candidate looks at the opponent who has just called his clearly shaky "facts" into question and says, "Are you questioning my integrity?" *Well*, I want to say to this politician, *since I find I have to question my own integrity quite often, I find it hard to trust a man who never questions his.*

At the annual shareholders meeting, the CEO gives his "State of the Company" assessment in a speech that tells "the good" and neglects to include "the bad, and the ugly." At first it sounds plausible, as if he has represented the facts exactly as they are. Then, after the meeting, you look at the faces in the hallway and you see a different story. Their expressions tell it loud and clear: "What company was he describing? It definitely wasn't the one I belong to!"

There are two things going on in the above scenarios. First, these leaders are telling the truth, but they are not telling the whole truth… and everyone knows it. Second, they are not telling the truth about the fact that they aren't telling the whole truth.

In the physical world, if something is pure, that means it has no impurities. Take drinking water or a pane of glass, for instance. When these things are pure, you can see right through them. They are transparent.

The truth is that no one likes to be completely transparent. Everyone fears exposure. So we hide what we don't want others to see and we hold back when we think our self-disclosure could harm us in any way. We all agree integrity is important, but almost no one admits that it is a struggle at our very core. But in order to have integrity, the first thing we must do is admit that we don't have perfect integrity.

What did that last sentence do for you? I hope you found it refreshing. I hope you felt a little relief that the key to integrity is not to get it perfectly right all the time. It's to be transparent.

I have found that the most difficult place to be transparent in business is with prospects and clients. That's because of the unavoidable, unspoken agenda in every meeting. We may pretend it doesn't exist, but we all know it's there. We may posture and pose around it, but our customers see it and we see it:

If they buy, we make money.

So how do you pursue integrity when this agenda is so tightly woven into your business context? I believe integrity will develop in our lives when all the previous virtues work in concert:

- Humility, where we have assembled gifted people to provide value.
- Empathy, where we are emotionally connected with the customer so that we really care about addressing their issues.
- Attentiveness, so that we are really listening to what they want.
- Accountability, so that we will be careful about what we promise.
- Acceptance, so that even if we don't hear what we want to hear from the customer, we meet them where they are now.

If these virtues are increasingly in place in your life, real integrity is possible.

My dad is the best example of integrity that I know. He was a supervisor of an automobile assembly plant, responsible for negotiating contracts with the United Autoworkers Unions. These were high stakes deals, millions could be lost, and my dad approached the negotiating table with patience and honesty. Over time, he earned the right to say things others wouldn't dream of saying simply by applying the virtues consistently in all his relationships, including in business.

The bottom line in business is tri-fold. There is a deal to be done, that deal must include a deliverable promise, and that promise must in some way be a win-win transaction. All of this is contingent upon your ability to articulate a good value proposition to your customer. If you know your value proposition is strong, you will find it easier to be transparent.

Think about it. If you cannot identify and communicate a strong value proposition, why did you get in front of the customer in the first place? If you don't have a strong value proposition, your starting premise is dishonest. You're saying, "I do not really have a valuable proposal that can benefit you. I am simply here because I need the money!"

Components of a Compelling Value Proposition

Buyer motivation falls into two primary categories: financial (more measurable) and artistic (more emotional). By financial I mean that through buying the service or product, customers can improve their financial position. By artistic I mean that by purchasing the service or product, they gain something of a more aesthetic quality – it makes them feel better about themselves, or their lifestyle will be less stressful, or their home becomes more beautiful. Usually, a good value proposition will capture both of these motivational categories.

Here is an example of financial motivation in my business: "If you hire us for $50,000, we anticipate being able to *decrease* your asset management fees in a range of $100,000 per year over the next five years, totaling up to $500,000."

Add the following element to it, and you'll get a feel for the artistic motivation of a deal: "We will also set up a systematic process that will make your life easier and develop a consistent message to plan participants that will move them to greater levels of retirement readiness."

It's part of your job to determine how to tilt your presentation along the continuum of financial and artistic motivations. Because this is such a delicate balance, never the same for any one client or customer, this will be a skill you'll continually hone throughout your career.

But you're not done yet. Your value proposition may have integrity, but is your presentation credible? A big part of your value proposition will be discovered as you are interacting with your prospective client. Once they have disclosed their needs and wants, you should articulate back to them what you heard. Then you state your intention to deliver what they want. At this stage, you are gaining the necessary credibility and achieving what I call trusted advisor status. When you have gained this level of trust, your focus moves to, "How can I respond in a way that is worthy of the trust given to me."

Here's the thing. Everyone knows any deal worth its salt is going to be a struggle to pull off. Everyone knows that nothing, absolutely nothing, of any value is a quick fix. Almost everyone suspects that you, like every other member of the human race, have had your share of failures and struggles. If you want to have real transparency and credibility, admit it.

Let's go back to an example I mentioned previously. "If you hire us for $50,000, we anticipate being able to decrease your asset management fees in a range of $100,000 per year over the next five years, totaling up to $500,000."

Here is the struggle, honestly communicated to the client: "Up until a few years ago, we would not be confident that we could do this for you even though we have been in the retirement plan business for years. We felt like we were doing good work but here is what we did not have":

The team assembled to pull this off:

1. An experienced investment advisory person using a proven investment due diligence process.

2. A fiduciary management person who had the compliance experience.

"We will also set up a systematic process that will make your life easier and develop a consistent message to plan participants that will move them to greater levels of retirement readiness."

"Again up until a few years ago we lacked the proper systems. And we believe it is impossible to pull this off without good systems":

1. For investment due diligence we use our *Scorecard System.*

2. For fiduciary management we use our *Fiduciary Briefcase* and *Benchmarking Analysis Report.*

"Even with all of this to guide us, we are not perfect. Most of this work is going to be done by people on my team rather than myself.

When we occasionally make a mistake, we are committed to owning up to it. At the end of the day, we think this is the kind of advisory relationship you need and we believe you are going to enjoy working with us."

Personal Outcome from Integrity: Transparency

Surprise people and be vulnerable. Be open. Go ahead and discuss how those very failures in the past positioned you to know what you're talking about today. Go ahead and divulge the price you've paid before. While you're at it, don't take all the credit for the amazing deal that's about to go down. Go ahead and admit that you will be delivering on the promised result with the help of the other gifted people on your team.

I often discover that in business situations, when I am transparent with clients, they are often transparent in return. They tell me what they need, and often I am able to assist them in their buying process. I have discovered that business, which can be just a mechanical function in life, becomes filled with a certain magic and mystery when I enter every meeting, every transaction, and every conversation with every person as myself.

Business Outcome from Integrity: Credibility

What does integrity look like in business? In sales situations, for example, be proud of your product's benefits and be candid about its limitations. When you do, you garner trust with the customer and cause them more likely to do business with you than the competition.

When presenting your business to potential investors, talk about what's in it for them, but also tell them about the hard work, struggles, and risks involved to achieve the financial returns you propose. This will enhance your profile and credibility in the eyes of those investors.

Your credibility is also important in leading your employees. They need to hear from you that the career and the lifestyle they can achieve with you exceeds what they can find elsewhere, but they also need to know how difficult it is going to be to achieve it. This is a value proposition that has integrity and is credible.

Questions for Application

Where have you seen an obvious lack of integrity in the news lately?

Do you feel the freedom to be yourself? Why or why not? Take the risk and be transparent about this.

How would your organization score in a Transparency Index?[14] If you think you'd have a low score, how can you change that?

---

[14] Zach Silberman, "And the Winner for Transparency is...MCC," October 24, 2013, http://www.usglc.org/2013/10/24/and-the-winner-for-transparency-is-mcc/

CHAPTER 9
Virtue #7:
Peacemaking vs. Territorialism

How to Handle Conflict

A "silo effect" is a broad business term for an insular management system where reciprocation is nonexistent. For example, a business may lack coordination in all of its marketing techniques so that they support each other and continue to move a prospective client through the marketing system. Alternatively, an organization's efforts at creating cross-selling opportunities with their existing client base are thwarted by divisions within the company that aren't willing to risk their position with the client. Everyone agrees that the silo effect is a dysfunctional and inefficient model; yet, not many companies examine the vice that often contributes to the issue. Maybe that's because, on some level, it's a vice we all practice. I call it territorialism.

Some degree of territorialism is a natural instinct. It feels safe to guard what we have. However, when individuals or divisions in your company "guard their turf" or don't share information, seeds of distrust and even anger are sown.

You probably see it all the time. One person is offended by another. The offended party, instead of confronting the offender, talks to everyone else, and you can bet what he's saying is not positive. People choose sides, and before you know it an entire office is riddled with dysfunction and rancor.

When the vice of territorialism is in full force, only its opposite virtue, peacemaking, can counteract the problem. Peacemakers work to restore peace in a relationship when it is broken. They're willing to risk their position in an effort to confront the problem and work on a resolution. They refuse to give a bad report of another person without first going to the source and working with them on resolving the conflict.

Territorialism is the standard operating procedure of our day, whereas peacemaking is quite rare. The reason it is so rare is that the peacemakers often take the heat in their efforts and suffer the consequences, at least in the short run. Personal issues are not easily resolved and it takes lots of energy and perseverance. The confident people who commit to this virtue find themselves in a highly functional environment.

A person who exemplifies the virtue of peacemaking goes directly to the person with whom the disagreement or offense has occurred *in private* as soon as possible and expresses how he/she feels about the matter. He, as Steven Covey suggests, listens in order to understand.[15] Sometimes this process leads to immediate reconciliation while at other times things cannot be worked out. Occasionally reconciliation unfolds over a long period. I have experienced this with everyone in our firm at one time or another and in turn, each has experienced this with me.

When I am initially confronted with a situation, my first thoughts are emotionally charged and aimed at proving how wrong the other person is on the issue. But everything is different if I'll confront them in a spirit of peace having first examined myself. Diplomacy and grace kick in, and I begin to see another perspective on the situation. I have seen this work with clients who have unrealistic expectations or when we may have dropped the ball. It takes a great deal of vulnerability to be a peacemaker. Making peace and restoring relationships is difficult work and often more of a lifelong pursuit, rather than a onetime event.

Peacemakers leverage their negative experiences for the good of others, sometimes with very powerful results. Olaudah Equiano, former slave and famous author, dedicated the latter part of his life to peacemaking. Equiano was a strong proponent of the abolition movement in England. Although he experienced the brutality of slavery firsthand, having been kidnapped in Nigeria, shipped the West Indies, and on to the British colony of Virginia, Olaudah

---

[15] Stephen Covey, "Habit 5: Seek First to Understand, Then to be Understood," *www.stephencovey.com*, https://www.stephencovey.com/7habits/7habits-habit5.php.

chose to use the freedom he eventually purchased to help bring about the end of slavery in England.[16]

The Elusiveness of Peace

"Why?" I asked one of our strategic partners about a client who'd dropped us after six years of nurturing our relationship with him.

"Because they were unhappy with us."

"When did you hear about this?"

"A while back."

"What were they unhappy with?" I asked, wondering why I hadn't heard one whiff of this before now.

What I did hear was the rumbling of bus tires about to flatten me. "They didn't say specifically," he said, "but I told them I'd handle things from here."

You'll handle it, all right, I thought, *I'd like to handle you.*

Do you blame me? And can you blame me for tossing and turning that night, for entertaining, just a few thoughts of revenge? This man saw an opportunity to cut us out, and he took it.

---

[16] Olaudah Equiano, "The Interesting Narrative Life of Olaudah Equiano or Gustavus Vassa, the African, Written by Himself," March 17, 2005, http://www.gutenberg.org/files/15399/15399-h/15399-h.htm

Territorialism comes easily to me. And why not? I worked hard to acquire this client and in some way I considered him "ours." Judging by my reaction to the news that he'd been taken from us, it's pretty clear I'd been standing guard over my acquisition. This stance does not make for peace, either in my own heart or in my business. So how can I instead guard my heart from territorialism? By becoming a peacemaker.

Personal Outcome of Peacemaking: Authenticity

Conflict prevention is best done on the front end of any relationship whether it is with a strategic partner, an employee, or even a prospective client. It is good to specify the exact parameters of an arrangement in writing before you get started as a way to head off conflict before it happens. Map out who is responsible for what and when and how the revenue sharing is going to work.

I also think it is important to have some sort of commitment to common values in writing. This is why we have started laying *The Great 8* vice/virtues octagon on the table for discussion and agreement. This at least lays a foundation of how to work together.

Most business leaders I know are men and women of action, and I'm no exception. I consider this a good quality, but in my haste to act I often run right into an unnecessary and unanticipated conflict. I have learned that I need to contemplate before I act…specifically; I need to do this contemplation for a little longer than my instincts tell me is necessary. I need to slow down and think, stop, and pray.

Conflict is a little like death and taxes. No matter how hard we try, it is unavoidable. But avoiding conflict (which is very different from preventing it) is exactly what most of us do. We almost never go to the person who wronged us. Instead we find someone else, someone unrelated to the conflict, and we vent to him or her. This sideways communication might feel good at the moment, but it does absolutely nothing to solve the problem.

Conflict resolution is not easy. That's because no one likes to apologize or forgive. It's awkward and painful. We don't forgive and we don't give others the opportunity to forgive us. In fact, rather than forgive, most of us suffer the offenses of others in silence, leaving big, gaping holes in our relationships.

But it doesn't have to be this way.

1. Go to the person who has wronged you.

2. If that doesn't work, take someone with you to mediate.

3. It's the only way to maintain an authentic relationship!

As hard as it is to achieve in business, peacemaking is sometimes even harder with friends and family. In business if things do not work out with a strategic partner or an employee, separations occur and everyone goes his/her own way with relatively light repercussions. With lifetime friends it can be a painful process. Sometimes making the first move in peacemaking is a bite-the-bullet kind of thing. You have to do it if you're going to sustain the relationship.

Of course in families the stakes are even higher. As our family has grown, we have had to use a combination of one-on-one conversations or family meetings to get these misunderstandings worked out. It's never fun, almost always painful, but it always makes the relationships more authentic afterward.

Business Outcome from Peacemaking: Stronger Team

Team building may help prevent conflict, but it is not just about that. It is about forging stronger relationships in the context of your team. There are as many ways to build your team as there are team members. Working together and living out the virtues helps build a team. But it cannot be all work. There has to be some time for "hanging out" and just being together. Maybe it's having a meal where you don't talk business. Maybe it's some other recreational activity – golf or fishing or whatever works for the unique people with unique interests on your team. It's time to relax a little and just be in the moment.

Team building may not seem like a big deal, but trust me it is. It creates a culture of family and friendship in your business like nothing else can. It enables your people to find other ways to connect in ways that can possibly sustain a relationship when it walks through the fire of a conflict. *The pressure of conflict, when it's resolved by applying the virtue of peacemaking, can produce the multi-faceted diamond of an amazing team.*

Forgiveness Creates Peace

Forgiveness does not come naturally to me, but it can be done. Less than one week after the phone call with the partner I wrote about earlier in this chapter (the one who in my opinion threw me under the bus), I received a text from him. He wanted to "clear the air." Had that call come earlier in the week, I would have thought, "Yeah right, we'll see about that."

We met in my office for about twenty minutes. He apologized for not handling things well. I told him I not only forgave him, but I released him from any debt to me and we weren't talking chump change. This was his largest marquee client, an international company you would recognize if I revealed the name. So I guess you could say it was a miracle that I was able to genuinely forgive him.

But the real miracle came afterward. I told him I thought he looked good and that I'd been concerned about him when I'd seen him last on the West coast. I even said I thought his countenance had been dark. He confided in me that he had been angry with his ex-wife back then, that the bitterness had been eating him up. Even though he tried to reconcile with her after their divorce, she wanted nothing to do with him. He was now remarried, but struggling. "My wife does so many things that really irritate me," he said.

In the short span of our conversation I moved from offended business partner to friend, confidant, and counselor. I shared some hard-won wisdom from my own marriage, and he expressed his appreciation.

Questions for Application

What's the difference between healthy ownership and unhealthy territorialism? How have you experienced both?

What did you learn about conflict resolution in this chapter that you can apply the next time you face conflict? How do you think this information will improve your relationships overall?

Do you have a strong team? How might intentionally leaning into conflict grow your team?

CHAPTER 10
Virtue #8: Courage vs. Fear

Keeping the Faith in the Midst of Change

In the world of financial markets, there's always something to fear. However, fear is more universal than that. Everyone, from the child who refuses to go to the dark basement to the entrepreneur poised to spend millions of his investor's money; everyone knows what it's like to be frozen in fear – to allow the thing ahead of us to paralyze our judgment and our resolve so that we're stuck.

No one understood this kind of fear more literally than the crew of the *Endurance*, Ernest Shackleton's ship that set sail for the Antarctic in 1915. The men lived on ice, literally, for almost two years. They survived while waiting for the ice floe that held their ship in the clutches of the Weddell Sea to loosen its death grip. Fourteen months of waiting for the thaw of spring…and freedom. But in the end, the ice had its way. The men endured. The ship didn't. Next stop: two months on a large, flat floe that eventually broke in two and necessitated a journey to nearby Elephant

Island. Five harrowing days in three open lifeboats across a frigid sea. Once his crew was safely ensconced on the island, Shackleton made one of many courageous decisions. He gathered five men and set off in the strongest of the three lifeboats for South Georgia 800 miles away. If they were to be rescued, they would have to go get their rescuers. It was a daring and heroic mission, and it certainly wasn't an infallible one. For 105 days, the remaining crew waited for the return of "the Boss." Their hope had odds stacked against it like towering glaciers. By the time Shackleton returned in a borrowed Chilean vessel, the 22 men had a mere four-day's supply of food left. If that.

Shackleton's courage overcame the vice of fear; a vice that could have sunk the *Endurance* had its captain not chosen to act bravely each time the situation needed such an action.

As G. K. Chesterton wrote: "Courage is almost a contradiction in terms. It means a strong desire to live taking the form of a readiness to die. A soldier surrounded by enemies, if he is to cut his way out, needs to combine a strong desire for living with a strange carelessness about dying."[17]

Ultimately, we must find the strength to be courageous and live out these virtues in the face of stiff opposition. It is often amazing to see how strong the battle lines become when opposition comes against us. It really is a battle.

---

[17] G.K. Chesterton, "Orthodoxy," *www.gutenberg.org*, http://www.gutenberg.org/cache/epub/130/pg130.html.

In business, we face a different kind of battle. Perhaps you were overlooked for a particular assignment. You can feel persecuted when you spend hundreds of hours and thousands of dollars pursuing a new customer opportunity and they do not choose you.

What happens when rejection comes and defeat looks imminent? We are forced to ask the question, "Why am I doing this anyway?" The answer has to be more than making money. We think we need more money, but what we actually need is more life.

Confronting Fear with Faith

Let's say you've just encountered a fresh new business idea, and you're certain you'd like to pursue it. You're jazzed about the idea and then you do the numbers. You calculate the risk. This is often where fear kicks in. You begin to think how certain people in your organization might resist. You begin thinking, "What happens if this doesn't work? What if I'm too late? What if this idea becomes obsolete before I can put it into action?" You begin to visualize your failure before you've even begun. The fear of change can slow you down in your efforts to effect change. It can even paralyze you.

Courage is not instinctive. So how do we operate consistently in courage instead of fear? How do we stay there? Occasionally I make a little headway. A few Saturday nights ago I went to bed in a foul mood and awoke a different man.

During the night, as I dreamed and fretted (I honestly don't know how much was dreaming and how much was fretting), it suddenly became clear to me that the reason for my bad mood was fear. I wasn't afraid of any one thing in particular. I felt a ubiquitous anxiety about everything. I was worried about my wife, Anne, about the children, the grandchildren, the business, friendships, and ministry. Everything that was important to me was wrapped in fear.

I don't particularly enjoy fear. But I have discovered that real courage cannot take hold unless we are first gut-level honest about our fears. I began to talk to myself. I became both exhorter and heckler in the audience, and the following argument ensued.

"We have always succeeded in the past! Why would I ever doubt?"

"But what if such and such happens?" cynical, fearful me said back.

On and on. You get the idea.

I reached a turning point during the night. Remember in our session about acceptance, I wrote about "proclaiming the truth in advance?" Well, it turns out this is a great way to tip the scale toward courage when you are wracked with fear.

"You know what?" I decided in the middle of the night, "I am going to expect good outcomes on all of this! Looking back over my life, Providence has always come through for us in ways we would never dreamed could happen. I am blessed beyond measure."

I began to rehearse all of the issues I was worried about in my head and to visualize positive outcomes according to what I perceived to be the best path. I didn't ignore the dangers, the possibility of surprises and hardships, but I refused to dwell on anything on the basis of my fear.

Courage is far more than an effective sleep aid for those of us who tend to fret late at night. In July 2011, my friend and business partner, Bill Straub gathered the leaders of our organization together for lunch and told us he had pancreatic cancer. He told Marc, Denise, and me something none of us will ever forget, "I don't know whether or not I have days, months, or years left; but no matter what happens to me, you guys have got to keep Legacy going." Bill had just heard the worst news a person could hear, and he wasn't thinking of himself. He was thinking of us, not about his future, but ours. This was courage.

I met Bill back in 1978 when I first entered the financial services business after a three-year career in teaching and coaching. Bill was the top producer in the firm – the big dog. When I started in the insurance business, I called on all of my friends and acquaintances. I remember standing at the counter in our office where other sales people brought applications for processing. I watched them line up and wondered, "Am I ever going to have an application to submit?" Bill walked up to me at one point and asked me how things were going. I said, "I've contacted a lot of people, but nobody's buying."

His next question seemed like a no-brainer: "Are you asking them to buy?"

I had to think long and hard about that one. The honest answer was no, I hadn't. I admitted that I was afraid of rejection and worried about what people thought about me. After some serious soul searching, I was determined not to let fear stop me from doing what needed to be done. So, to make a long story short, I, like Bill, became successful in the insurance business.

Fast-forward the next twenty-one years to 1999, during which time Bill and I had a friendly competition for the top spot in the agency. However, on one particular day our relationship started down a different road together. Bill and I were having lunch swapping ideas about how we could become better in the business. At the end of our lunch, we both agreed we could never be in business together because we both had such strong personalities. However, six months later, I called him to join me and two other colleagues who were going into business together. During that year we worked on all the necessary plans to launch a new business. Right before we went to sign the five-year lease for our first office space, Bill called me.

I heard the anxiety in his voice before he could get one sentence out. "David," he said "I have to tell you; I am scared to death!"

I suggested we get together the next day to talk. We met in a private room at a business club near our homes. Bill poured out his heart to me, and I quickly realized this was about more than a business decision. I learned more about him in those three hours than I had known about him in the previous twenty years. As he talked about his failures and struggles, it was clear to me that Bill was searching for deeper answers. For peace.

My talk with Bill that day reminds me of Forrest Gump. If you recall, Forrest and Lieutenant Dan started a shrimping business together, and at first it struggled. The roiling ocean scenes symbolized Lieutenant Dan's anger with God over this and all his other failures. He was definitely not at peace with God, or with anyone. Forrest summed up the resolution Dan experienced like this: "I guess you could say Lieutenant Dan found his peace with God."

That's exactly what Bill found and I could relate. I'd found a real, lasting peace with God when I was sixteen. Peace with God had carried me through every up and down of life since then, and I watched as it carried Bill from that point forward. The two of us connected that day at the business club, and we became comrades and blood bothers for life.

Early in our business, we gathered everyone in the firm together for a retreat. One night we watched the movie Butch Cassidy and the Sundance Kid. Chase scenes abound in the movie, with funny and tragic outcomes. During one scene in particular, when Butch and Sundance couldn't seem to elude their pursuers with their usual tricks, they looked over their shoulders several times and said, "Who are those guys?" They were the enemy, but Butch and Sundance couldn't help but respect them.

We decided that's what we wanted people to say about us. "Who are those guys?"

We wanted to stay with people through thick and thin and to be authentic. We were determined to show the world we were different from the people who promised big and delivered small. We wanted to be known for our relentless follow-through.

As in most partnerships, Bill and I did not always agree on things, and we had some fierce conversations over the years, loud and fierce at times. We were always able to find common ground. Eventually, every time, one of us would apologize and ask for forgiveness. Then we would go on a sales call together and things would click, and we'd end up having a great meeting. During those times, Bill would say to me, "Butch, you did good." Then he would ask, "How do you think I did?" I would say, "You did good Sundance - real good!"

Bill lived about 19 months after his cancer diagnosis. During that time, he was intentional about staying engaged with all of the people in his life who mattered to him. Bill really did "fight the good fight." Almost every workday for thirteen years, Bill and I had at least one conversation a day. My last conversation with Bill was the day he passed away. I didn't know if he could hear me or not, but I said what was on my heart anyway: "Bill, very soon you are going to be in a much better place, and it won't be long before the rest of us are going to be there too! Until that time, we are going to carry on the work that we all started together. The Legacy must go on."

And it will.

Personal Outcome from Courage: Faith

Faith means visualizing the fulfillment of a worthy goal. The function of faith is to act as if this goal has already been achieved. This is the kind of faith that sustained the crewmembers of the Endurance. Their journals paint a picture of an organized life in which decisions were made daily to keep everyone's spirits up. These dairies read like letters home from summer camp. Shackleton encouraged ice football, sing-a-longs, and storytelling. They had few books, so they read aloud to each other. The men listened to a recipe from their one cookbook every night and discussed ways they might improve the dish. It took faith to create a culture like this on a literally sinking ship.

Shackleton's enemy was the ice that trapped his ship. But the real enemy was fear. One can only imagine the many ways fear reared its ugly head on that ship.

The enemy that causes many business leaders to shrink back in fear is criticism. It can become a cycle. You demonstrate strong leadership by standing firm on your convictions, even when those convictions are unpopular. You will incur criticism, which, naturally, makes taking a stand the next time to be a fearful proposition. No one would invite criticism (at least not most people), but for the leader it is inevitable. Faith is the hopeful trait that can get you through the icy waters of criticism and resistance.

Business Outcome from Courage: Effective Change Management

At the heart of Shackleton's leadership was an ability to manage change and to do it repeatedly as circumstances shifted like icebergs in a warming ocean. Had Ernest Shackleton nursed an aversion to change, one can only imagine the fate of his crew. In a similar, if less dramatic way, corporations must keep up with the dizzying pace of change if they are going to succeed.

Change like this can be exhilarating, but it often leaves behind a wake of fear in employees, customers, and investors. In order to avoid the debilitating effect of fear, company leadership must demonstrate a great deal of intestinal fortitude to keep things on track. One of my advisory board members recently said courage is the number one virtue business leaders need today in order to be good at the business competency of change management.

The other virtues certainly come in handy here. Without empathy to solicit the concerns and, yes, fears of others, without acceptance of those employees, without humility to consider changes you didn't devise, and without accountability to keep the right decisions in play, change cannot be managed as it should in a corporate environment. Courage, without the other virtues, can be a buzz saw instead of a scalpel. Change can be unnecessarily bloody. When working in tandem with the other virtues, courage can have epic outcomes. Just ask the crew of the *Endurance*.

Questions for Application

What enemies do you fear most and why? Have you made any headway in battling those enemies with courage?

Imagine a fearful or worrisome circumstance in your life. How can you exercise faith? What outcomes do you hope for and explain what they would look like if they actually happened?

What change do you anticipate in your organization in the next few years? How can you face these changes with courage? How might the other virtues equip you for change?

CHAPTER 11
The Unifying Source

Putting it All Together

One sentence, just three little one-syllable words, is quite possibly the most recognized tagline in branding history. I say Nike and you say...

Just do it.

Even the most sedentary couch potato alive knows the mantra and has maybe even chanted it out loud in a brief attempt at self-motivation.

Just do it.

I have to admit I love that phrase. I like the way it sounds, the images of purposeful action it evokes, the way I feel pumped when

I hear it spoken aloud. I mean, it's brilliant. This one short sentence is, in itself, a blur of grace and motion.

When I invited you on this journey to discover and embrace *The Great 8* virtues, I confess this was the value proposition I had in my head. We were going to just do it together, and the end result would be that we all ended up, together, at the same bottom line. Maybe you're like me, and you naturally gravitate to this kind of bottom line thinking, the kind that is easily fueled by a catchy, upbeat slogan and focuses with laser-like intensity on the end results.

Here's another confession: In my excitement about the future, I forgot to ask the most important question of all. I forgot to ask why.

Maybe the bottom line needs to be examined for us to really get it right. I'm discovering that when I stop and ask why, I get to a more satisfying, sustainable goal. Sure, I love results as much as the next guy, but I am learning that we cannot adequately define the bottom line unless we ask why.

The Why

Simon Sinek suggests in his book *Start with Why* that people will be inspired by your message or your product if you can find and communicate your why. He cites Apple, whose message wasn't, "We develop computers and other technology that is exceptional" but rather, "We want to change the world."[18]

---

[18] Simon Sinek, "Start with Why (Penguin Books Ltd: 2009).

We don't buy Apple products because they're cool; we buy them because Apple has a compelling reason for making them. A reason most anyone can appreciate on some level. Who doesn't want to change the world?

But I have to ask: Why are we inspired by the question *why*?

Clearly, once you start asking why, you can almost always ask it again.

Why am I on this earth?

The answer to that question needs to be asked!

The most important aspect of *The Great 8* is the culture of trust and vulnerability that flows from them. We succeed when we are able to share our hearts with each other. Part of that is sharing our fears and concerns, but an equally important art is sharing our dreams and visions. Not all dreams and visions are necessarily good. Some people come up with very harmful ideas, but within the context of *The Great 8* – the dreams and visions have to be good for all concerned. I believe dreams and visions in this context have a divine source and that makes all the difference.

The following are some of the benefits of aligning with *The Great 8*:

- We have a clearer picture of ultimate reality. Reality is what is true, and truth is a good thing. The message is clearly about creating meaningful experiences in the workplace and relationally connecting to others. If this is true, every aspect of our lives should be aligned with this.

- **Humility** or self-giving, is a foundational virtue. It is the foundation of leadership and of all the other virtues. It enables a leader to appreciate the gifts of others on the team. When a leader leads with humility, the sum of parts of a team become greater than any single person or leader on that team.

- **Empathy** enables a leader to emotionally connect with others, especially when the leaders knows and appreciates the individual stories that are unfolding in the lives of the people around him or her.

- **Attentiveness** enables a leader to be focused in the present moment with others and to serve them in excellent fashion.

- **Accountability** enables leaders to stay on the right track in the correct way with the sincere motives because they have invited others to speak the truth into their lives.

- **Acceptance** enables a leader to see the emerging giftedness in a person. It also enables that leader to proclaim the truth in advance in such a way that the people he or she leads are encouraged to fulfill the pursuit of their dreams.

- **Integrity** requires that we identify a strong value proposition for whomever we serve. If we're confident we are delivering value, we can be transparent on all of the "sticky issues" involving compensation for the work we may do for them.

- **Peacemaking** requires that we keep short accounts with people. We don't let hurt feelings fester. If things get off track relationally, we examine ourselves first, and then we go directly to the person and gently work toward reconciliation.

- **Courage** requires that we keep the why we are here in the first place and continue to envision the fulfillment of the dreams placed on our hearts.

Do you see what I see here?

The virtues are not, in themselves, the bottom line. The positive outcomes associated with them are not the bottom line, either. These act as road signs to show us we are on the right path, steadily moving toward the Source.

The virtues remind us to go back to Him when we fail because we will never reach perfection. As long as we live in our temporary bodies here on earth, there will always be a tension between the virtues and the vices. We will always feel the tug of our own imperfections.

Do you see how rich life becomes when the how (aligning every aspect of life with the eight virtues) is tethered to the why? The pursuit of our individual and collective dreams within the context of *The Great 8* is urging us toward a great story, one in which we are continually aligning every part of our lives, including work and business. Additionally, we can trust that, as our individual stories expand and overlap with others, they will be orchestrated into an unfathomably larger story.

SUMMARY

When people in any organization work together toward a common goal, we have discovered eight vices that have a degenerative effect on the group. Most groups lack relational capital, the equity that accrues over time as people experience life events, where they display trust for each other.

Because of this, most strategic business relationships do not last long enough to become successful. We have discovered eight corresponding virtues that counteract the negative effect of each vice. An awareness and openness to these virtues among the members of a group, builds trust and teamwork – thus the relational capital needed to build long-term success.

Adherence to the virtues creates an environment that provides a better view of reality with the way things are, not as they appear to be.

1. Humility/Egotism – Humility, realizing and valuing the gifts of others within a group and working to keep each person's ego in check.

2. Empathy/Busyness – Empathy, the ability to share in what others are feeling requires that we prioritize work assignments in a way that allows time for personal interaction and relationship building.

3. Attentiveness/Distraction – Attentiveness, being engaged fully to all aspects of the present moment requires us to eliminate distractive communication, so we can focus on the mission at hand.

4. Accountability/Greed – Accountability, giving permission to others to ask the question, "Is this right?" Because greed is the unjust pursuit of personal gain to the exclusion of others and each person must be able to answer to every other person within the group in order to overcome the vice of greed.

5. Acceptance/Anger – Acceptance, meeting people where they are, not where we expect them to be counteracts the tendency to get angry and cut off a relationship.

6. Integrity/Dishonesty – Integrity, being transparent and avoiding the temptation to create a better picture of ourselves than is justified counteracts our tendency toward self-deception.

7. Peacemaking/Territorialism – Peacemaking, resolving personal conflicts as quickly as possible can overcome an "us versus them" mentality that causes territorial dysfunction within the group.

8. Courage/Fear – Courage, the ability to visualize a successful outcome when confronted with the risk of loss, pain or uncertainty, enables the group to overcome the debilitating effect of fear.

ABOUT THE AUTHOR

DAVID HARPER serves as President and CEO of Legacy Advisory Partners which is a national consulting firm that works with companies to assess, implement, and measure ROI opportunities on their human capital.

He is a graduate of Davidson College where he was a Division I quarterback and ranked 3rd nationally in passing in 1973. David did post-graduate studies at Furman University and Georgia State University. David has served on the Board of the Good Samaritan Health Center and currently serves on the Atlanta Project Young Life Committee. He and his wife, Anne, authored the book "Light Their Fire for God" (developing virtues in your children) published by Moody Press and released in 2001. They have three married children and ten grandchildren.

CONTACT INFORMATION

J. David Harper, Jr.

Legacy Advisory Partners

11175 Cicero Drive, Suite 100

Alpharetta, Georgia 30022

Cell (404) 435-0635

dharper@lebllc.com www.lebllc.com

Made in the USA
San Bernardino, CA
31 August 2016